Helping Johnny Listen

Helping Johnny Listen

Taking Full Advantage of the Sermons We Hear

THADEUS L. BERGMEIER

WIPF & STOCK · Eugene, Oregon

HELPING JOHNNY LISTEN
Taking Full Advantage of the Sermons We Hear

Copyright © 2010 Thadeus L. Bergmeier. All rights reserved. Except for brief quotations in critical publications or reviews, no part of this book may be reproduced in any manner without prior written permission from the publisher. Write: Permissions, Wipf and Stock Publishers, 199 W. 8th Ave., Suite 3, Eugene, OR 97401.

Wipf & Stock
An Imprint of Wipf and Stock Publishers
199 W. 8th Ave., Suite 3
Eugene, OR 97401
www.wipfandstock.com

ISBN 13: 978-1-60899-383-3
Manufactured in the U.S.A.

Scripture quotations taken from the New American Standard Bible®, Copyright © 1960, 1962, 1963, 1968, 1971, 1972, 1973, 1975, 1977, 1995 by The Lockman Foundation Used by permission." (www.Lockman.org)

To all the faithful preachers of God's word every week across our globe, may this book help increase the fruit of your ministries as your people are molded into better listeners to God's sermons through your mouths.

Contents

Preface ix
Introduction xi

1 The Preaching Intersection 1

2 Receive the Preaching of God's Word 27

3 Examine the Preaching of God's Word 66

4 Live the Preaching of God's Word 100

5 Persevere the Preaching of God's Word 127

Conclusion 151
Bibliography 155

Preface

In 1966, Rudolf Flesch wrote *Why Johnny Can't Read: and what you can do about it*. His point in writing this book was mostly to give advice on how to help people read. Over time, many books have been written concerning Johnny. He has not been able to write, tell the difference between right and wrong, add, concentrate, sell, brand ideas, preach, and many more things. Over the years, Johnny has stood for a mythical character of the average person, both male and female.

I have entitled this book, *Helping Johnny Listen*, because I am not so concerned with the problems the average person experiences in listening to the preaching of God's Word. I am concerned with helping them become the listeners that God created them to be. My concern as I write is the common individual in the common seat at the common church. I want to help this common individual think through responsibilities and activities they can engage in so that when the Word of God is preached, they are able to hear the words that God has for them. It is my aim to help people who listen to sermons to get the most from what they hear. Hence the subtitle: *Taking Full Advantage of the Sermons We Hear*.

The book begins with the connection between preaching and listening. I have called it the preaching intersection. The purpose of this chapter is to raise the awareness of the need of preaching and if preaching, then listening. Chapter 2 deals with what happens before the preaching event. Chapter 3 deals with ways to listen with an ear towards the discernment of the truth. In my estimation, Chapter 4 is the most important because listening is ultimately fulfilled when the person responds to the words of the sermon. The last chapter deals with common obstacles that seem to keep the listener from fulfilling their duty to the sermon.

Most of this research was done for a Doctorate of Ministries program through Baptist Bible Seminary in Clarks Summit, Pennsylvania. I would be remiss if I did not acknowledge all of my professors for their help thinking through many of these issues. In particular are Dr. Don McCall and President Jim Jeffery.

To Dr. Sandy, you have made this text readable, thank you for your help.

To Bryan Hodge, a college friend, thank you for convincing me to have this published.

To those at my church, Grace Bible Church in Hutchinson, Kansas, who have sat through many lectures and sermons, I am grateful to you and your continual response to the word of God preached. Specifically for those who have read it and given feedback: Jodi Fish, Curt Thompson, and my pastor, Rick Goertzen.

As with most people, I am a result of the influence of my parents, so thank you. In particular I am indebted to my mother, who taught me the English language. I apologize for the mistakes that you, and not many others, will see.

To Monique, Karsten, JT, and Anni, thank you for allowing me time away to complete this project. Thank you for your patience, your grace, and your willingness to share me with the church. I love you all and pray that as you children get older, you will mature to become effective listeners to God's word preached.

Most importantly, to my Lord Jesus. It has only been through your grace and mercy that this book has been completed. Thank you for accomplishing salvation through which we can now hear your voice through the voice of our preachers.

Introduction

THIS BOOK IS FOR Christians. This book is for Christians who concern themselves with God's word. This book is for Christians who concern themselves with the preaching of God's word. If that is you, you need to read this book. If it is not you, do not waste your time; rather, find people who fit that description and give the book to them.

Over the past several years, there has been a wealth of material calling pastors back to their God-given responsibility to preach his word without shame or embarrassment. Yet, there is relatively little information addressed to the people in the church as they sit under the weekly preaching of the word of God. How are they to listen to the preaching of God's word? What are they to do when the Bible is preached to them the way God intended preaching to take place? How are people to respond to biblical preaching?

I will never forget the first time I considered this problem. I was sitting at a national conference for pastors, looking out at over 3,000 men who were receiving instructions on going back to their churches and preaching more boldly, accurately, and passionately. I sat there thinking that their people have no idea of what is about to hit them next week. Their people have no concept of what it means to respond to the preaching they are soon to receive. Their people need to understand what it means to listen to preaching from God's word. At that moment, I felt a burden for the people who sit in the pews every week. Michael Fabarez accurately noted:

> The average preacher has spent thousands of hours reading, attending classes, learning biblical languages, and honing skills in order to communicate the life-changing Word of God in an effective way. The average congregation, on the other hand, has received little or no training on how to listen to and integrate the sermons they hear each week . . . There are no seminars, workshops, or conferences designed to prepare your audience on how to receive the life-changing messages you proclaim

week after week. This is amazing when you consider that the Bible gives more instruction on how to receive God's truth properly than it gives on how to proclaim it properly. God is very concerned with how preachers preach. But we tend to neglect His concern with how listeners listen.[1]

It is my general contention that people who call themselves Christian struggle to listen to the preaching of God's word. The listening problem extends much deeper than just being church related; it is, in fact, a problem that can be traced to being human. Certainly there are some people who have developed good listening skills; but generally speaking, people do not listen well. The problem with listening started at the very beginning of time when Adam and Eve failed to listen to God giving instructions concerning what they could or could not eat. Since that time, inherent in mankind is the natural tendency not to listen, not to respond. Ask the wife who tries to talk to her husband while he is watching a football game. Ask the parents who try to talk to their child to explain how to take out the garbage. Finally, ask the pastor who continually preaches God's word while looking at a crowd that is sleepy, distracted, disinterested, or immune to his words. People have a listening problem!

Dr. Ralph Nichols has often been called the "father of listening," and a significant amount of information about the process of listening in the field of education today has been credited to him from research he conducted at the University of Minnesota in the 1960s and 1970s. He made this observation about listening:

> Behind the widespread inability to listen lies what, in my opinion, is a major oversight in our system of classroom instruction. We have focused our attention upon reading, considering it the primary medium by which we learn, and we have practically forgotten the art of listening. About six years are devoted to formal reading instruction in our school systems. Little emphasis is placed on speaking, and almost no attention has been given to the skill of listening. Listening training—if you could possibly call it training—has often consisted of a long series of admonitions extending from the first grade through college: "Pay attention!" "Now get this!" "Open up your ears!" "Listen!"[2]

---

1. Fabarez, *Preaching That Changes Lives*, 151–52.
2. Nichols and Stevens, *Are You Listening*, 10–11.

He was correct in his assessment of the educational classroom, probably even conservative. Students are taught from an early age the importance of writing and reading. Much of the educational classroom experience is given to learning letters, forming sentences, and sounding out vowels; and rightly, it should be. Reading and writing are vitally important. Even when children reach secondary education, they are taught for a few years the art of speaking. Yet how often are students taught to listen?

Although human beings in general are not good listeners in any subject, attempting to listen to someone preach from the Bible is even harder. It is harder because of the spiritual dynamic that is taking place when the preacher stands up to preach. As the Apostle Paul said, "Our struggle is not against flesh and blood, but against the rulers, against the powers, against the world forces of this darkness, against the spiritual forces of wickedness in the heavenly places" (Eph 6:11–12). The preaching event is unlike any other speaking event, for the audience must deal not only with the physical liabilities of listening but also with a spiritual battle that is taking place in which their natural sinful condition does not want them to change and neither does the enemy of Christ. To be effective listeners to preaching, individuals must have all the abilities of the person who listens to the president of the United States give the State of the Union address; but they must also have the resolve of someone striving to be like Jesus spiritually. This is something that happens multiple times a week in the lives of Christians who are faithful in attending church where they hear several sermons a week.

One word of clarification may be helpful at this point. Is there a difference between *hearing, listening,* and *obeying*? According to Merriam-Webster[3], the differences between these terms are slight yet very important. Hearing is defined as "the process, function, or power of perceiving sound; specifically, the special sense by which noises and tones are received as stimuli." Listening is defined as "to pay attention to sound; to hear something with thoughtful attention, give consideration." Obeying is defined as "to follow the commands or guidance of." At least in the English language, these terms are used as steps in a process: Something is first heard. Then when it is given attention or given consideration, it is said to have been listened to. That produces action or obedience. Listening, then, is the hinge upon which hearing becomes obedience. Throughout this book, the term *listen* will be used

---

3. http://www.merriam-webster.com, (accessed, January 28, 2010).

in this sense: "hearing something that produces obedience." It will be impossible to talk about listening to sermons if the assumption is not made that what has been heard in that sermon makes an impact upon the person, which results in change in that individual's life.

Reflecting on the beginning of man, how was Adam and Eve's failure to listen manifested? Their failure to listen was evidenced in the fact that they did not obey what God had told them to do. What is found in the Scriptures is a clear connection between listening to God's truth and obeying what it says. That is the purpose of this book: to help Christians, who concern themselves with God's word being preached, get the most out of each sermon they listen to so that they can have maximum life change.

I write this not from some ivory tower looking down on listeners, but as a person who sits in the pew next to them. I get to preach often, but the majority of my time in church is spent in the pew. This book contains principles that I have tried to work out in my own life over the course of the last fifteen years of sitting under godly preachers who faithfully brought forth God's word each and every week with the goal of seeing life change in me. For that, I am forever thankful. The preachers I have sat under and the preachers I know take tremendous responsibility in this process, but it is time for the listeners to take some responsibility as well. It is time for those who listen to sermons to understand better their responsibility in listening to their preachers, to their sermons, and ultimately to God.

This is not something to gloss over or something that should be ignored. There are too many people in churches who mean well but are poor listeners. There are too many people in churches who have never been taught what it means to develop good listening skills, particularly when sermons are preached. The church is one generation away from being like the nation of Israel, as God described them to the prophet Ezekiel,

> But as for you, son of man, your fellow citizens who talk about you by the walls and in the doorways of the houses, speak to one another, each to his brother, saying, "Come now and hear what the message is which comes forth from the Lord." They come to you as people come, and sit before you as My people and hear your words, but they do not do them, for they do the lustful desires expressed by their mouth, and their heart goes after their

gain. "Behold, you are to them like a sensual song by one who has a beautiful voice and plays well on an instrument; for they hear your words but they do not practice them." (Ezek 33:30–32)

It is time for the preacher's sermon to be more than just elevator music. Some say that we are already there, that for many people the preacher is like background noise in their lives. But there is hope for the church. There is hope if people are taught what it means to listen properly and effectively to the preaching of God's word. To that end, this book has been written.

1

The Preaching Intersection

PREACHERS ARE TO PREACH! Listeners are to listen! When the preacher and listener work in harmony with each other, something special happens. Preaching is never to be one-way communication. Most people can look back over their church experiences and quickly note favorite sermons. In most cases, those favorite sermons are ones in which the persons listened faithfully to preachers who faithfully preached God's word. However, all preachers can look back to times they failed to preach as they should have; and all listeners can look back to times they failed to listen as they should have.

The theory of this chapter is that when one of the parties involved in the preaching event fails to accomplish that person's goal, the preaching event is not what it should be. In the preaching intersection, how the preacher and the listener intersect, God still speaks through what he has spoken through his Holy Scriptures; and, as the preacher and listener work in harmony with each other, the words of God are able to be heard and understood.

There is something unique about the oral presentation of the message of the gospel truth that God uses to transform people. The gift of preaching is the anointing of a messenger who has faithfully used God's word to give a specific message to a specific group of people. The Apostle Paul recounted his experience with such a group of people in the city of Thessalonica: "For this reason we also constantly thank God that when you received the word of God which you heard from us, you accepted it not as the word of men, but for what it really is, the word of God, which also performs its work in you who believe" (1 Thess 2:13). What these people received was the word of God preached to them. Leon Morris was accurate when he said,

> Fundamental to Paul's preaching was the conviction that what he spoke was not his own message but God's. He rejected human wisdom and thought little of mere eloquence. He was content to pass on, in the manner of a herald, what God had given him ... His drive and forcefulness came not from some thought that he was abreast of contemporary trends in philosophy or religion or science, but from the deep-seated conviction that he was God's mouthpiece, and that what he spoke was the veritable word of God.[1]

When preachers are faithful in opening the Bible and explaining the book by telling what it has to say about the lives of the listeners, the words that they lay out for the listeners are exactly what God has to say. This needs to be made abundantly clear: The preacher is not what is powerful; the message is. When a preacher is faithful to preach the message from God's word, it is as if God is speaking to that audience; and the listeners, when the Bible is preached, are placed at a crossroad with every sermon. That is why Paul said he was a "fragrance of Christ to God among those who are being saved and among those who are perishing; to the one an aroma from death to death, to the other an aroma from life to life" (2 Cor 2:15–16). As listeners listen to a biblical sermon, the message means life to some and death to others. That is a heavy responsibility and is the reason the preaching intersection is so important.

At this point, there are usually two questions. The first deals with the listener: *If the listener does not listen, is God still speaking?* This is the proverbial "if a tree fell in a forest and nobody was around to hear it, did it make a sound?" argument. But the answer has to be yes! God is still speaking! He has promised that his word will not return empty (Isa 55:11). God is still speaking through the preaching of his word even if nobody is listening.

The second question has to do with the preacher: *If the preacher does not preach the Bible, is God still speaking?* This question will be addressed more adequately later in the theology of preaching, but the short answer has to be no! God is not speaking through a preacher's anecdotal stories, clever outlines, funny illustrations, or tear-jerking accounts of life. God speaks only when the preacher does his job of opening, explaining, and applying the Bible. God is heard only when the listener does his job and listens. When those two things intersect, real preaching takes place and God speaks through that which he has spoken in the Bible. The rest of

---

1. Morris, *First and Second Epistles*, 79.

this chapter reveals how these conclusions were reached through a theology of preaching and preachers and a theology of listening and listeners, showing how both must intersect to accomplish what God wants to accomplish through the biblical sermon.

A THEOLOGY OF PREACHING AND PREACHERS

Mile Marker #1: God Preaches!

Foundational to a theology of preaching is the fact that God is the first preacher. God is not some sort of silent being living in the universe and leaving mankind alone. He is not, as a deist might believe, a god that created the world, set it in motion, then allowed mankind to know him only if they used their reason to figure him out. In contrast, God is actively involved in the life of the known world; and one of the main ways God is involved in the world is through his communicating himself. He has preached. He has revealed himself to his creation. God communicating to people is a hallmark of biblical Christianity. The God of the Bible is continually contrasted to the false gods of the world because they cannot speak: "Why should the nations say, "Where, now, is their God?" But our God is in the heavens; He does whatever He pleases. Their idols are silver and gold, the work of man's hands. They have mouths, but they cannot speak; they have eyes, but they cannot see; they have ears, but they cannot hear; they have noses, but they cannot smell; they have hands, but they cannot feel; they have feet, but they cannot walk; they cannot make a sound with their throat" (Ps 115:2–7; see Hab 2:18–19).

The Apostle Paul told the people of Corinth that before Christ, they were "led astray to the mute idols" (1 Cor 12:2). J. I. Packer stated, "For, though God is a great king, it is not his wish to live at a distance from his subjects. Rather the reverse: he made us with the intention that he and we might walk together forever in a love-relationship. But such a relationship can only exist when the parties involved know something of each other. God, our Maker, knows all about us before we say anything (Ps 139:1–4); *but we can know nothing about him unless he tells us.*"[2]

There are at least four sermons that God preached.

First, God preached creation. From the very first pages of Scripture, it becomes obvious that, in a sermon-like manner, God preached to bring

---

2. Packer, *Knowing God*, 110. (emphasis mine)

about the creation of this world. Sixteen times in Genesis 1, God records that he communicated with word his purpose and plan for creation. At the beginning of each day, Genesis says, "Then God said." From that moment, creation speaks about God and continues to this day to be a message to everyone that he exists. The psalmist said that God's sermon created the world and speaks of his glory. "By the word of the LORD the heavens were made, and by the breath of His mouth all their host. He gathers the waters of the sea together as a heap; He lays up the deeps in storehouses. Let all the earth fear the LORD; let all the inhabitants of the world stand in awe of Him. For He spoke, and it was done; He commanded, and it stood fast" (Ps 33:6–9; see Ps 19:1–6).

Charles Haddon Spurgeon is famous for saying that the "sun, moon, and stars are God's traveling preachers."[3] This is because everywhere they go, they tell about God; and they go everywhere on this earth. The Apostle Paul even spoke about God's sermon of creation, that that message makes mankind to be without excuse (Rom 1:20). This first sermon by God is one that allows mankind to understand the wonderfulness of God and creates in man's heart a hunger and thirst for something greater than himself.

Second, God preached the law. When did God first communicate his law? Surprising to some, it was not up on the mountain with Moses; it was in the garden with Adam that God first spoke, giving specific instructions: "From any tree of the garden you may eat freely; but from the tree of the knowledge of good and evil you shall not eat, for in the day that you eat from it you will surely die" (Gen 2:16–17). God adequately and succinctly communicated to mankind the manner in which he would have them live. The only restriction was the portion of the sermon that Adam failed to obey adequately. When the serpent appeared, what did he say? According to Genesis 3:1, the crafty serpent said, "Indeed, has God said, 'You shall not eat from any tree of the garden'?" In his own little sermon, Satan questioned the message of God. Eve (and then Adam) believed the sermon of Satan instead of the sermon of God about what was best for them. Thus, sin entered the world.

Throughout Genesis, God communicated several times with explicit instructions for his people: to Noah in building an ark, to Abram in moving to a new land, to Abraham in sacrificing Isaac, and to Jacob (Israel) in taking his family down to Egypt. In all these occasions and

---

3. Spurgeon, *Treasury of David*, 127.

many more, God was speaking, or one might say preaching, his purpose and will for the person to whom he was talking.

God did eventually give what is known as the Law to Moses. Up on that mountain, Moses received the specific law that the people of Israel were to follow. It started with these words: "Then God spoke all these words, saying," (Exod 20:1). What proceeded were not only the Ten Commandments but also the exact instructions on how God would have his people live. God spoke these commands for the people of Israel so that they would be separate from other nations. What happened? Throughout the rest of the Old Testament, his people struggled with keeping the law. That is why in the New Testament, Paul said that the purpose of the law is to lead people to realize that they need help, to be a tutor pointing to Christ (Gal 3:10–14, 23–29). God preached the law so that mankind know they need help, which ultimately comes in his third sermon.

Third, God preached Jesus. The author of Hebrews put this sermon in these terms: "God, after He spoke long ago to the fathers in the prophets in many portions and in many ways, in these last days has spoken to us in His Son, whom He appointed heir of all things, through whom also He made the world" (Heb 1:1–2). Throughout the Old Testament, God spoke through prophets in many ways: through dreams, visions, and audible voices and sometimes through angels. But his last communication was through his son, Jesus Christ. He preached his Son. The Apostle John said, "In the beginning was the Word, and the Word was with God, and the Word was God" (John 1:1). Later he wrote, "The Word became flesh, and dwelt among us, and we saw His glory, glory as of the only begotten from the Father, full of grace and truth" (John 1:14). It is apparent that the Word here is a reference to Jesus Christ. But what is meant by the term *Word*? The reformer, John Calvin, said concerning this term applied to Jesus, "The evangelist calls the Son of God the Word simply because, first, he is the eternal wisdom and will of God; and secondly, because he is the exact image of God's purpose. Just as men's speech is called the expression of their thoughts, so it is not inappropriate to say that God expresses himself to us by his speech or Word."[4]

Interestingly, God used this term to say that his ultimate message to mankind is a physical sermon in the person and work of Jesus Christ. As the Apostle John later wrote, "No one has seen God at any time; the

---

4. Calvin, *John*, 13.

only begotten God who is in the bosom of the Father, He has explained Him" (John 1:18). Jesus became God's living sermon.

Fourth, God preached the Bible. God wrote the Bible and explained how he did it. In 2 Timothy 3:16–17, the Apostle Paul wrote, "All Scripture is inspired by God and profitable for teaching, for reproof, for correction, for training in righteousness; so that the man of God may be adequate, equipped for every good work." When it says "all Scripture is inspired by God," it means that it is "breathed out by God." This term comes from a compound word, *theos* ("God") and *pneustos* ("to breathe out or blow"). Literally, it has the idea that all Scripture is breathed out by God. Robert Saucy said, "In using this term, the Apostle was not declaring that the Scriptures were breathed into by God but that they are the product of the breath of God. They are in some sense God-breathed writings."[5] What that means is that God did not take a book that was written and breathed into it divine truth; he breathed out exactly what he wanted written for mankind to know about him. Of course, he did this through the means of a human element, using the personalities and styles of men. These men were not dictated to, nor were they illuminated with some special illumination that made everything they wrote inspired. They were God's instruments for his sermon of the Scriptures.

The Scriptures are first of all and above all from God and about Jesus. From Genesis to Revelation, God has revealed his truth, his character, his attributes, and his divine plan for the redemption of mankind whom God says is created in his own image. The Bible is God's sermon of Jesus put in written form so that those who were not alive at that time in history can still know him. Jay Adams said, "It is as much God's Word as if it were spoken audibly from His own mouth. If you were literally to hear God's voice, He would say nothing more, nothing less, and nothing different from what He has said in that Book. It is to be read, heard, and obeyed as fully as any literally breathed out words of God would be."[6] This great sermon of the Bible is as much the voice of God as it would be if God were to literally appear and read it to any individual. So, God preached creation, the law, Jesus, and his word. A theology of preaching and preachers must start here, for preachers preach because their God is a preacher. But he did not stop with his sermons.

---

5. Saucy, *Bible*, 44.
6. Adams, *How to Help*, 26.

Mile Marker #2: God Calls Preachers

Throughout the history of the world, God has called a variety of instruments to be the preachers of his message. God used an angel to communicate to Abraham just before sacrificing his son (Gen 22:11-12). God used Gabriel to preach a shocking message to an unknown virgin girl named Mary (Luke 1:26-33). God also used an angel in a vision to Cornelius to get him to summon Peter to him (Acts 10:3-6). There are many examples in the Scriptures of God using angels to preach for him. However, those are not the most unique messengers God has called to preach. In Numbers 22:22-30, God opened the mouth of a donkey to be his messenger. The most interesting part of that account is that when the donkey actually spoke to Balaam, he answered. Why he did not fall off the donkey in shock will always be a mystery.

Although angels and animals were extraordinary messengers of God, the more ordinary mouthpieces of God were called prophets. Throughout the Old Testament, God's message was proclaimed by men he had chosen and given a special message to preach: "I will raise up a prophet from among their countrymen like you, and I will put My words in his mouth, and he shall speak to them all that I command him. It shall come about that whoever will not listen to My words which he shall speak in My name, I Myself will require it of him" (Deut 18:18-19).

As the prophet said, "Thus says the Lord," it was just as if the Lord was preaching it to the people. The Lord put the words into the prophets' mouths. They preached God's messages as God's instruments. One of the clearest word pictures of this was when the Lord called Ezekiel to be his prophet. In a very peculiar exchange, the Lord told Ezekiel to eat a scroll; so he opened his mouth and was fed a scroll of God's words. Afterward God commanded him, "Son of man, go to the house of Israel and speak with My words to them" (Ezek 3:4).

What about today? What do the Scriptures say about today? Generally speaking, the Scriptures are clear that God now calls all Christians to be his preachers. This may sound surprising to most, but it is true. All Christians are called to be God's preachers to share the truth of Jesus with others. We learn from the Apostle Paul, "How then will they call on Him in whom they have not believed? How will they believe in Him whom they have not heard? And how will they hear without a preacher?" (Rom 10:14). John MacArthur commented, "Paul is saying that if God did not send preachers no one could hear, if no one could hear no one could believe, if no one could believe no one could call on the Lord, and if no one could call on Him no one could be saved."[7] All Christians are called to preach the name of Jesus to everyone with whom they come in contact so that his name will be exalted. It should be exciting that God wants to use people in the process.

Although all Christians generally are called to preach, God specifically calls certain people to be preachers. There is a difference between being called to preach and being called to be a preacher. One way to explain this is to look at everyday sporting examples. Is there a difference in playing golf and being a golfer? Is there a difference in playing football and being a football player? Is there a difference in hunting and being a hunter? Obviously, the former are activities that persons may enjoy doing; the latter are their lives. They are everything to these individuals, mostly because they work hard at them and have some sort of special ability to accomplish that which they are.

A clear example of this distinction is found in Acts 8:4–5: "Therefore, those who had been scattered went about *preaching* the word. Philip went down to the city of Samaria and began *proclaiming* Christ to them" (emphasis mine). Those who were scattered went about preaching the word, which is the term *euaggelizo* meaning "to announce good news." Philip went down to Samaria and was proclaiming Christ, which is the term *kerusso*, meaning "to herald or proclaim." D. Martyn Lloyd-Jones said, "That is the position then, that every Christian should be capable of doing what is indicated in the fourth verse, but that only some are called upon to do what is indicated in the fifth verse. In the New Testament this distinction is drawn very clearly; certain people only are set apart and called upon to deliver the message, as it were, on behalf of the Church in an official manner."[8] The point is that God has given some a gift of communicating the Bible to people. He has called some people to be preachers.

Mile Marker #3: God Commissions Preachers

When God gifts certain men to be preachers, he commissions them to take seriously their calling to be preachers. This is no trivial thing. There are several commissions that God gives to the preachers He calls.

---

7. MacArthur, *Romans 9–16*, 83.
8. Lloyd-Jones, *Preaching & Preachers*, 102–03.

First, God commissions the preacher to live the word of God. If the man of God is to be a preacher of God's word, he must first and foremost be someone who lives and exemplifies the word of God in his character. Jones again said,

> What does the Church look for in a man who says that he is called to be a preacher? Obviously she must look for something exceptional in him. He must be a Christian of course, but there must be something more, there must be something additional. What do you look for? Well, you remember how in Acts 6, even in the matter of appointing deacons, who were simply to handle a financial problem, a charitable matter of feeding widows, it was insisted upon that they should be men "filled with the Spirit." That is the first and greatest qualification . . . What else do you desiderate? You now proceed to look at what we commonly call character. I would not describe "being filled with the Spirit" as character, which means that he is a man who is characterised [sic] by a godly life.[9]

The Lord placed qualifications upon the leadership of an overseer or pastor (1 Tim 3; Titus 1). In these chapters, Paul gave twenty-one characteristics that the pastor is to be known for and all but one of them has to do with his character. This shows that God cares more for who the preacher is than for what he can do. It does not mean that the preacher is perfect but that he is above reproach in all those qualifications. It means that he leads the way by example of the message that he is preaching. The preacher is to watch his life closely (1 Tim 4:15–16). Character counts for the preacher. He is to live the word of God. He is to be a visible representation that God is still actively alive and working and speaking. Charles Spurgeon in his book, *Lectures to My Students*, said,

> We do not trust those persons who have two faces, nor will men believe in those whose verbal and practical testimonies are contradictory. As actions, according to the proverb, speak louder than words, so an ill life will effectually drown the voice of the most eloquent ministry. After all, our truest building must be performed with our hands; our characters must be more persuasive than our speech. Here I would not alone warn you of sins of commission, but of sins of omission. Too many preachers forget

---

9. Ibid., 109–10.

to serve God when they are out of the pulpit, their lives are negatively inconsistent.[10]

He is saying that God commissions preachers to live the word of God!

Second, God commissions preachers to cut the word of God. The concept of cutting the word of God is found in 2 Timothy 2:15, where God tells his man to "be diligent to present yourself approved to God as a workman who does not need to be ashamed, accurately handling the word of truth." Does the preacher come to the Scriptures with a flippant attitude or does he take the task of preaching seriously? The concept of cutting the word of God comes from the phrase "accurately handling the Word of Truth." It is a phrase that means to cut along a straight line. Kent Hughes said,

> Being one who "correctly handles" the Word requires getting it straight and giving it straight. "Correctly handles" has as its basis the Greek word *orthos* ("straight"), the same word from which we build words like *orthopedic* and *orthodoxy*. The exact charge to Timothy is to "impart the word of truth *without deviation, straight, undiluted.*" Here it refers to the straight, precise, careful communication of the word of truth, the gospel . . . This apostolic command to get it and give it straight has become a 2,000-year-old charge to all who are called to teach and preach the gospel.[11]

It is a similar concept in anyone's trade, whether it is carpentry or medicine or business or education. Whatever the trades, one hopes the individuals want to do them to the best of their abilities so that they are correct and not found to be wrong. They want to cut straight lines so that whatever they do is not found to be crooked. This is what Paul is talking about, taking the responsibility so seriously that the preacher gets it right. Why is that necessary? Can't God still use the message even if the preacher does not get the passage right? He can, but that does not mean that he does. Getting the message right is of utmost importance. Understanding the Bible correctly is critical. Individuals who do not understand it correctly will not be able to teach it correctly. Preachers are to handle accurately the word of God, to cut it straight so that when they preach that straight word, their audiences of listeners can listen in the same manner. If the preachers get it wrong, the audiences will get it

---

10. Spurgeon, *Lectures to My Students*, 17.
11. Hughes and Chapell, *Timothy and Titus*, 209.

wrong. All preachers show their views of God's word through the way they handle the word when they preach.

Third, God commissions preachers to re-oralize the word of God. Preachers are to take that which was once preached by God and written down onto paper and repreach it. They are to make the message of God audible once again. One of the main Greek terms for preaching in the New Testament is *kerusso*, which has a sense of proclaiming. It is oral. It is the person shouting from the rooftops. Preachers are not to share, discuss, or have conversations but are to preach or proclaim the message of God's word. Samuel Logan said, "Preaching communicates the force of the Bible as no other way of handling it does . . . To preach them is thus no more, just as it is no less, than to acknowledge them for what they are, and to let their content be to us what it already is in itself. The Bible text is the real preacher, and the role of the man in the pulpit or the counseling conversation is simply to let the passages say their piece through him."[12]

Paul told his dear friend Timothy, "I solemnly charge you in the presence of God and of Christ Jesus, who is to judge the living and the dead, and by His appearing and His kingdom: preach the word; be ready in season and out of season; reprove, rebuke, exhort, with great patience and instruction" (2 Tim 4:1–2). He was commanded to preach the word. Do the terms *reprove*, *rebuke*, and *exhort* sound like this is a quiet ordeal? Of course not! It is meant to be something like the prophets used to do in the Old Testament, telling the people that God has a word for them. That is why preachers often get worked up. They are shouting and screaming what God would have for us to do. They are re-oralizing the Scriptures.

Preaching has a bad rap these days. Many claim it is too offensive. It is too harsh. It does not help people work through their issues. It is not interactive enough. It should be a conversation. Many preachers in the church have taken the term preach and changed it to *talk*. They say, "My talk this morning is about_____." Sorry, but a theology of preaching says that preachers are to model themselves after God, the first preacher. Did God converse when he preached creation? Did he converse to see what humans might think about the idea of Jesus being the incarnate word? No, he preached or proclaimed these things, and he modeled biblical

---

12. Logan, *Preacher and Preaching*, 17.

preaching. Albert Mohler, president of The Southern Baptist Theological Seminary, said,

> Ultimately, preaching will cease to be Christian preaching if the preacher loses confidence in the authority of the Bible as the Word of God and in the power of the spoken word to communicate the saving and transforming message of the Bible. The preacher must stand up and speak with confidence, declaring the Word of God to a congregation that is bombarded with hundreds of thousands of words each week, many of them delivered with a sound track or moving images. The audacious claim of Christian preaching is that the faithful declaration of the Word of God, spoken through the preacher's voice, is even more powerful than anything music or image can deliver.[13]

Biblical preaching is simply the proclamation of the Scriptures to a group of people for the purpose of calling them to change something in their lives. Martin Lloyd-Jones defined preaching as "a transaction between the preacher and the listener."[14] More specifically, he said,

> Any true definition of preaching must say that that man is there to deliver the message of God, a message from God to those people. If you prefer the language of Paul, he is "an ambassador for Christ." That is what he is. He has been sent, he is a commissioned person, and he is standing there as the mouthpiece of God and of Christ to address these people. In other words he is not there merely to talk to them, he is not there to entertain them. He is there—and I want to emphasise this—to do something to those people; he is there to produce results of various kinds, he is there to influence people. He is not merely to influence a part of them; he is not only to influence their minds, or only their emotions, or merely to bring pressure to bear upon their wills and to induce them to some kind of activity. He is there to deal with the whole person; and his preaching is meant to affect the whole person at the very centre of life. Preaching should make such a difference to a man who is listening that he is never the same again.[15]

Preaching deals with the whole person. When preachers stand up to preach, they are trying to vocalize what a certain text means and to apply it to a group of people. The listeners sitting there are trying to

13. Mohler *He Is Not Silent*, 17.
14. Lloyd-Jones, *Preaching & Preachers*, 53.
15. Ibid., 53.

listen to God, not to their preachers. This is why a theology of preaching is so important for listeners to understand. They need to understand that there is a transaction taking place between their preachers and them and that their preachers are trying to change something in their listeners' lives: "The communication is to be understood neither in physical terms (from pulpit to pew), nor even in human terms (one mouth speaking, many ears listening), but in divine terms (God speaking through his minister to his people)."[16] When preachers are faithful to the text of the Bible and preach the text and not themselves, it is as if God is speaking to their audiences during those sermons. In the re-oralizing of the text, God speaks.

Fourth, God calls preachers to serve the word of God. This is a very important distinction: Preachers are to bow their knees to the Scriptures; the Scriptures do not bow to the preachers. Preachers are to serve the word of God, not serve the shifting thoughts and feelings of some people.

After Paul called Timothy to preach the word in Second Timothy, he gave his reasoning: "For the time will come when they will not endure sound doctrine; but wanting to have their ears tickled, they will accumulate for themselves teachers in accordance to their own desires, and will turn away their ears from the truth and will turn aside to myths" (2 Tim 4:3–4). This is surely a statement against listeners, but it is also a shocking statement that there are some preachers who will change what they are preaching to have more and more people come to their churches. They will avoid any difficult sections of Scripture because they are offensive or harsh. They will refuse to deal with the hard words of the Bible. When Paul was leaving the Ephesian elders, he said that he did not shrink from declaring to them the whole purpose of God (Acts 20:25–27). Preachers must not shrink from saying the things that God wants said in his word so that they can tickle the ears of listeners who really do not want to listen to God but want to create imaginary gods in their minds.

Mile Marker #4: God Does His Work through His Spirit

God preaches, calls preachers, and commissions preachers to preach. All of that would be null and void if not for God sending his Spirit to help in the process. Preachers throughout the history of the church have

---

16. Stott, *Between Two Worlds*, 81–82.

acknowledged the need of the Holy Spirit in this process. Spurgeon said, "If there is to be a Divine result from God's Word, the Holy Ghost must go forth with it. As surely as God went before the children of Israel when He divided the Red Sea, as surely as He led them through the wilderness by the pillar of cloud and fire, so surely must the Lord's powerful presence go with His Word if there is to be any blessing from it."[17]

Jesus told His disciples that after he left, he was going to send the Holy Spirit to them. He calls him the Spirit of Truth and said that the Spirit "will not speak on His own initiative, but whatever He hears, He will speak; and He will disclose to you what is to come" (John 16:13). The doctrine of illumination is the Spirit of God opening the eyes of the believer to gain a fuller understanding of God's truth. It is a divine act whereby the person is now more readily able to understand the things of God.

Mohler said, "Both the preacher and the hearers are dependent upon the work of the Holy Spirit for any adequate understanding of the text."[18] When God does his work through the Spirit, he does it in two ways. He does it through preachers. Preachers need comprehension in the studying phase of the preaching process to cut the word of God straight. But God also does it through listeners. The only hope of the listener is for the Holy Spirit to take that which the ear hears and plant it into their heart.

It is on this road, this theology of preaching and preachers, that God speaks through that which he has already spoken. He does this when his men are faithful to his word. The question now is whether anybody is listening.

A THEOLOGY OF LISTENING AND LISTENERS

As already mentioned, Paul's commission to Timothy at the end of Second Timothy is a watershed passage for preachers to preach God's word unashamedly. There is a great responsibility for preachers, who stand under the accountability of God and Christ Jesus, who judge the living and the dead, to preach the word of God. Paul continued in that passage, talking about listeners who are looking to get their ears tickled. Therefore, one may wonder whether that same sort of accountability is

---

17. Spurgeon, *All-Round Ministry*, 339.
18. Mohler, *He Is Not Silent*, 45.

true of listeners. That is, do listeners also stand under the presence of God and Christ Jesus, who judge the living and the dead, for how they listen? Will God hold listeners accountable for their listening to the same degree that he will hold preachers accountable for their preaching?

In the Scriptures, there are more than 1,600 verses that refer to ears, hearing, listening, and other related terms. Many of those passages contain several occurrences per verse. Gathering data from these passages may help a person develop a theology of listening and listeners.

Some of the passages have nothing to do with listening; they deal with the ear and do not help in constructing a theology of listening. For instance, Exodus 21:6 does not help because it says, "Then his master shall bring him to God, then he shall bring him to the door or the doorpost. And his master shall pierce his ear with an awl; and he shall serve him permanently." This passage talks about the physical ear; it says nothing concerning listening. However, there are many verses about the ear that do give insight into this theological discipline. For instance, in Numbers 23:18–19, Balaam spoke on behalf of God as a messenger of God to Balak: "Arise, O Balak, and hear; Give ear to me, O son of Zippor! God is not a man, that He should lie, Nor a son of man, that He should repent; Has He said, and will He not do it? Or has He spoken, and will He not make it good?" *To give ear* means to give undivided attention to the message that is about to be spoken by the prophet. So, what does the Bible say about listening?

Mile Marker #1: God Created Ears So We Could Listen to Him

There should be no doubt in any Christian's mind that God created the human body and, in so doing, created the ear: "The hearing ear and the seeing eye, The LORD has made both of them" (Prov 20:12). Marveled by the human ear, theologian John Stott said,

> What a remarkable organ God has created in the human ear! In comparison with it, the most sophisticated computer (it has been said) is "as crude as a concrete mixer." Of course what we usually call the ear is only the *outer ear*, that fleshy excrescence on the side of the head which comes in a variety of shapes and sizes. From it a one-inch canal leads to the ear drum, behind which is the *middle ear*, where the body's three tiniest bones (popularly known as the anvil, the hammer, and the stirrup) amplify sound twenty-two times and pass it on to the *inner ear*, where the real hearing takes

place. Its main component is the snail-shaped tube named the cochlea. It contains thousands of microscopic, hairlike cells, each of which is tuned to one particular vibration. The vibrations are now converted into electric impulses which convey sound to the brain for decoding along 30,000 circuits of the auditory nerve, enough for a sizeable city's telephone service. The human ear has rightly been celebrated as a "triumph of miniaturization."[19]

When God created Adam in the garden, he gave him ears so that he could hear God. God wanted him to listen so that Adam could process, in the wonderful mind that God had given him, the instruction that God had for him.

There are other examples of God's purpose in the creation of the ear so that a person may hear from him. God made his covenant with David in 2 Samuel 7:18–22:

> Then David the king went in and sat before the LORD, and he said, "Who am I, O Lord GOD, and what is my house, that You have brought me this far? And yet this was insignificant in Your eyes, O Lord GOD, for You have spoken also of the house of Your servant concerning the distant future. And this is the custom of man, O Lord GOD. Again what more can David say to You? For You know Your servant, O Lord GOD! For the sake of Your word, and according to Your own heart, You have done all this greatness to let Your servant know. For this reason You are great, O Lord GOD; for there is none like You, and there is no God besides You, *according to all that we have heard with our ears.* (emphasis mine)

It was by means of the ears that David processed what he knew about God.

Jesus also repeatedly made the statement that the ears he created were to hear his message. One phrase is often repeated in the gospels by Jesus to his disciples: "He who has ears to hear, let him hear."[20] In addition, in the book of Revelation, after every message to the seven churches, Jesus says, "He who has an ear, let him hear what the Spirit says to the churches." Then it is said one last time in Revelation 13:9: "If anyone has an ear, let him hear." What is the purpose of these sixteen occurrences? It is to make the point that the ear is intended to be used

---

19. Stott, *Contemporary Christian*, 101–02.

20. Jesus does not always use the same construction, but the similar concept is constantly seen. See Matt 11:15; 13:9; 13:43; Mark 4:9, 23; 7:16; Luke 8:8; 14:35.

to listen to the message that God has. In his commentary on the book of Revelation, Robert Thomas remarked that "the mention of the 'ear' suggests an ability to perceive or understand. The one who possesses this ability is invited to pay special attention to what the Holy Spirit is saying to the churches in this particular message."[21]

In the English language there is a distinction between hearing and listening: they are steps in a process. People hear and then they listen. That difference is not as distinct in the Greek language, where almost exclusively the same term is used for hearing and listening. In the Old Testament, there are 1,028 occurrences of hearing and listening and their relative terms translated in the English version. Of those, 93 percent are the Hebrew term *shema*. In the New Testament, there are 445 occurrences of hearing and listening and their relative terms translated in the English version. Of those, all but six occurrences are the Greek term *akouo*. In the Septuagint, the Greek translation of the Hebrew Old Testament, the term *shema* is regularly translated with the Greek term *akouo*; they are seen as similar. Although there are shades of meaning, both of these terms are translated "hear" or "listen," depending on the context. There are some instances when they are only translated in the sense of sound perception, but the dominant sense in which they are used is that in which something spoken is to be heard or listened to and then obeyed. Speaking about the Greek term *akouo*, Colin Brown said, "The primary meaning is that of sense perception (e.g., the hearing of a trumpet, 2 Sam 15:10). However, apprehension is immediately involved as soon as one receives a statement, piece of news or message . . . Apprehension demands acceptance, listening . . . understanding . . . and attention to the thing heard.[22]

Why is it difficult in today's culture for us to comprehend, to listen, and to pay attention to that which we hear? If God ultimately made ears so that people may listen to him, why are we hard of hearing?

Mile Marker #2: Sin Has Destroyed Our Ability to Listen Effectively

Once Adam and Eve listened to the sermon by Satan instead of to the sermon by God, sin entered them. Now all mankind is sinful because of that event (Gen. 3:1–7). In theology, this concept is called total or

---

21. Thomas, *Revelation 1–7*, 151.
22. Brown, *New Testament Theology*, 173.

radical depravity. In Ephesians 2:1–3, all are said to be "dead" in their trespasses and sins. It says that humans are by "nature children of wrath." That means that as humans, people are not sick, ill, or partially hurt but are dead.

Parents never have to teach their children to do evil or to be bad, for it comes naturally to them. That precious newborn is so depraved that, if physically possible, the baby would proceed from the womb and slap mom in the face saying, "Give me some milk!" Steven J. Lawson said,

> All mankind is born spiritually dead in trespasses and sin. Fallen man is *totally* depraved. Sin has *radically* affected the *total* man. That is, each part of man—his mind, emotion, and will—is defiled by sin. His mind is darkened, rendering him unable to see the truth about God, Christ, or himself. His heart is defiled and does not desire God, but instead loves his sin. His will is dead and cannot choose what is right. Plagued with this total inability, sinners are in bondage to sin, unable to change and become good. Being dead in sin, man does not even desire to pursue what is right. In short, unregenerate man is totally unable to do any spiritual good, can do nothing to remove his sin, and can make no contribution toward his salvation. Worse, left to himself, fallen man will never seek God or His grace.[23]

One famous passage that deals with the depravity of mankind is Romans 3:10–18 in which Paul said that there are none righteous, there are none who seek after God. Left to ourselves, we would not want God and certainly would not want God to say something about how we should live. We want to be our own god.

When the Scriptures say that we are totally depraved, that means sin extends into every part of us; even to the core are we depraved. The heart is depraved and is against God. The eyes are depraved. The mind is depraved. And the ears, which God created for the purpose of listening to Him, are depraved. By nature, our ears do not want to listen to God. It is safe even to say that the ears are unable to understand God speaking to them. In Romans 3:11, Paul said "There is none who *understands*, there is none who seeks for God" (emphasis mine). This term *understanding* means "to set together" or "to gain insight." It is the step past listening and is usually used in conjunction with that term throughout the Bible. Individuals listen and then understand. It means that they listen

---

23. Lawson, *Foundations of Grace*, 34.

to the point that they get it; not only do they comprehend what is being said, but it means something to their lives. According to the *Theological Dictionary of the New Testament*, this term means "to perceive . . . primarily by hearing, to accept something by hearing and to follow it."[24]

In Romans 3, it says that there are none who understand. There are none who get God and his truth. There are none who have heard and have understood to the point that they are willing to obey what God is saying. There are none who by their own motivation will understand God. As MacArthur said, "Men are not sinful and hardened against God because they are ignorant of Him, but, to the contrary, they are ignorant of Him because of their sinful and hardened disposition."[25]

There is another place in the Scriptures where this term is used frequently, the famous parable of the sower in Matthew 13. In the first nine verses, Jesus gives the parable to his disciples, who fail to comprehend what he means by it. They come to Jesus and ask him why he speaks in parables. The purpose of verses 10–17 is to state to the disciples the reason Jesus tells them parables. In verse 13, Jesus says "Therefore I speak to them in parables; because while seeing they do not see, and while hearing they do not hear, nor do they understand." William Hendriksen noted that "though the sound of my voice penetrates their eardrums, and they catch enough of my meaning to become antagonized, they do not really understand and certainly do not heed, do not take to heart, my instructions, warnings, and invitations."[26] This is depravity. They fail to get it because of their radically depraved nature: "It is because the people have decided not to really see, hear, etc., as if this were a dreadful thing to do, that God has decided to punish them by allowing them to have their way!"[27]

Because of depravity, people see God and his truth as a threat to their lives, not as a hope for salvation. People may hear but do not listen or understand. They hear words, but they mean nothing. It is easy to comprehend what Paul meant when he said, "For *the word of the cross* is foolishness to those who are perishing, but to us who are being saved it is the power of God" (1 Cor 1:18, emphasis mine; in Paul's day, the word he referred to was a spoken word). People stand with blank stares on their

24. Friedrich, *Theological Dictionary*, 888.
25. MacArthur, *Romans 1–8*, 183.
26. Hendriksen, *Matthew*, 554.
27. Ibid., 556.

faces, saying "I just do not get it," or "I think I get it, but do not like it" or "That sermon makes no sense." Their depravity prevents them from hearing, listening, or understanding God.

Back to the soils identified in Matthew 13:18–23, Jesus explained that the seed that falls on the hard soil is "when anyone hears the word of the kingdom and does not understand it" (v.19). Conversely, "the one on whom seed was sown on the good soil, this is the man who hears the word and understands it" (v. 23). It is easy to see that those with hard hearts do not understand, while those with soft hearts do. The assumption as a person studies this text is that the seeds that fell on thorny and rocky soils are the persons who appear to understand but in the end are proven not to have understood.

This is the biggest problem in our lives: Sin has destroyed our ability to listen effectively to God. The Psalms give some insight into the heart of God, who wanted the nation of Israel to listen and understand:

> Hear, O My people, and I will admonish you; O Israel, if you would listen to Me! Let there be no strange god among you; nor shall you worship any foreign god. I, the LORD, am your God, Who brought you up from the land of Egypt; open your mouth wide and I will fill it. But My people did not listen to My voice, and Israel did not obey Me. So I gave them over to the stubbornness of their heart, to walk in their own devices. Oh that My people would listen to Me, that Israel would walk in My ways! (Ps 81:8–13)

Charles Spurgeon, commenting on this psalm, said, "What? Are the people so insensible as to be deaf to their God? So it would seem, for He earnestly asks a hearing. Are we not at times as careless and immovable . . . His warnings were rejected, His promises forgotten, His principles disregarded. Though the divine voice proposed nothing but good on an unparalleled scale of liberality, they turned aside."[28]

They were deaf to God because of their sin. Their sin caused them not to want to listen to God and not to want to hear from Him and not to want to obey Him. The prophets are great examples of men called to preach God's message to people who were not listening because they were choosing their sin over their God!

Look at the following examples, starting with Isaiah:

---

28. Spurgeon, *Treasury of David*, 714–15.

> Hear, you deaf! And look, you blind, that you may see. Who is blind but My servant, or so deaf as My messenger whom I send? Who is so blind as he that is at peace with Me, or so blind as the servant of the LORD? You have seen many things, but you do not observe them; *your ears are open, but none hears.* The LORD was pleased for His righteousness' sake to make the law great and glorious. But this is a people plundered and despoiled; all of them are trapped in caves, or are hidden away in prisons; they have become a prey with none to deliver them, and a spoil, with none to say, "Give them back!" Who among you will give ear to this? Who will give heed and listen hereafter? (Isa 42:18–23, emphasis mine)

Notice that their ears were open but they were not hearing.

Jeremiah's example could fill volumes about what it means not to listen because of hard heartedness; it is literally everywhere in his book. Jeremiah 6:10 says, "To whom shall I speak and give warning that they may hear? Behold, their ears are closed and they cannot listen. Behold, the word of the LORD has become a reproach to them; they have no delight in it." These people loved their sin more than anything, and it caused them not to hear the Lord. Later, Jeremiah preached God's message: "They did not listen to Me or incline their ear, but stiffened their neck; they did more evil than their fathers" (Jer 7:23–26).

The point is that sin keeps all people from hearing God as they need to hear him. It is interesting, though, that while sin keeps us from hearing God, hearing God is what we need to get rid of our sin problem. We find ourselves in a catch-22 that we cannot fix. We need God to do something first.

Mile Marker #3: Regeneration
Is the Key to Healing Our Listening Problem

The key to fixing any person's listening problem is found in the doctrine of regeneration. Regeneration is the work of God that changes a person's heart toward him. It is the giving of spiritual new birth. It is the same idea as being born again that Jesus told Nicodemus (John 3:3–8). In Titus 3:5, the Apostle Paul explained how salvation happens, that it is not by the works that individuals do but by the "washing of regeneration and renewing by the Holy Spirit." In talking about salvation, Peter said that individuals were "born again not of seed which is perishable but imperishable, that is, through the living and enduring

Word of God" (1 Pet 1:23). So Christians are born again according to the great mercy of God through the word of God.

The purpose of regeneration is to transform persons' hearts, once foolish, to the things of God and make them wise unto salvation. It is the necessary component of salvation that is accomplished by the Holy Spirit and through the word of God because of the mercy of God. This New Testament concept was talked about in the Old Testament: "Moreover, I will give you a new heart and put a new spirit within you; and I *will remove the heart of stone from your flesh and give you a heart of flesh*. I will put My Spirit within you and cause you to walk in My statutes, and you will be careful to observe My ordinances" (Ezek 36:26–27, emphasis mine).

We need to be born again. Now, the question often asked is how it happens. That is somewhat unclear from the Scriptures. Many people have used terms such as "effectual calling" or "irresistible grace." It is possibly helpful just for this purpose to think of it in these terms. Before salvation, one's eyes are blind and one's heart is dead to the things of God; or, to use the analogy of this book, the ears are deaf. A person has no desire for God, does not understand why people say he is so great, and fails to listen. But then the Holy Spirit comes and changes or gives a new heart, causing the person to be born again. The person opens the eyes to see God for who he really is. The person opens the ears to listen to him now. The person now sees clearly and says, "Wow, what a God. That's the glorious nature that people have been talking about. I see it now."

Paul said that the "natural man does not accept the things of the Spirit of God, for they are foolishness to him; and he cannot understand them, because they are spiritually appraised" (1 Cor 2:14). But the spiritual man can and does accept the things of God. I want to make this abundantly clear to the reader: The only way you will ever be able to listen to sermons is if you have been saved. There will never be a real heartfelt response to the Lord through the preaching of his word if you have never been converted. All that will follow will be worthless information to you if you do not first bow your knee to Jesus as your Lord and Savior.

That means you! Forget the rest of this book if you first do not know Jesus. Jesus Christ gave up the comfort of heaven, came to this earth, lived a perfect life, yet was sentenced to die a death of criminals. And he did, in fact, die a real, painful death. But three days later, he rose from the dead, proving once for all victory over sin and death. In doing this, he extended an invitation that your only hope of reconciliation, of a relationship with God, is through him. There is only one mediator, Jesus. He lived a life that you could not live, he died a death that you should have died, and he offers a gift that you cannot earn. Will you come to him today?

Maybe your issue with listening to the preacher is not that you are tired but that you are a sinner and have never dealt with your sin. Maybe your issue is not that the preacher is boring but that you are unconverted. Maybe the Bible seems dull and uninspiring because your ears are still plugged with your sin. My plea to you is to lay your sins at the feet of Jesus and be converted, or you will never hear the voice of God through the preached word.

This is such a real issue that Jesus said the only ones who listen to his voice are those who know him. As he rebuked the Pharisees in John 8:43–47, Jesus said,

> *Why do you not understand what I am saying? It is because you cannot hear My word.* You are of your father the devil, and you want to do the desires of your father. He was a murderer from the beginning, and does not stand in the truth because there is no truth in him. Whenever he speaks a lie, he speaks from his own nature, for he is a liar and the father of lies. But because I speak the truth, you do not believe Me. Which one of you convicts Me of sin? If I speak truth, why do you not believe Me? *He who is of God hears the words of God*; for this reason you do not hear them, because you are not of God. (emphasis mine)

Later in the book of John, Jesus said, "But you do not believe because you are not of My sheep. My sheep hear My voice, and I know them, and they follow Me" (John 10:26–27). Al Mohler said "God's true people are those who hear God speaking to them."[29] God's people listen to him. Those who are regenerated listen to him. That does not mean that they always listen perfectly, for they still have the residue of sin living in them, which they fight until glory; but they will listen.

That is what the rest of this book is about, how the regenerated person can get the most out of the preached word of God. Nobody will ever listen to God through the preaching of his word without first coming to Jesus. And for persons who believe in Jesus, listening to God's word being preached should mean something.

---

29. Mohler, *He Is Not Silent*, 58.

Mile Marker #4: The People of God Are Held Responsible for How Well They Listen to God

One thing is abundantly clear in the story of the Old Testament: The nation of Israel was not only to cherish the words of God but to listen and to depend on those words for everything that they were as a nation. The way in which they responded to God's word determined how God dealt with them. "God's people depend for their very lives on hearing His Word. For the Israelites, hearing God's Word and obeying it was a matter of life and death... For Israel, God's Word was like the manna in the wilderness. They needed it every day, fresh and new, if they were to survive at all. To hear the Word and obey it was life for them. Not to hear and not to obey would result in death."[30]

The book of Deuteronomy is quite an amazing story about the blessings that come with listening to God and the judgment that comes with not listening. For instance, Moses said, "Then it shall come about, because you listen to these judgments and keep and do them, that the LORD your God will keep with you His covenant and His lovingkindness which He swore to your forefathers" (Deut 7:12). Later he wrote, "Be careful to listen to all these words which I command you, so that it may be well with you and your sons after you forever, for you will be doing what is good and right in the sight of the LORD your God" (Deut 12:28). How seriously does God take his people listening to his voice? So seriously that blessing comes with listening to God and discipline comes with not listening to God. The story continued throughout the rest of the Old Testament, story after story of God's people either listening and being blessed or rejecting and being disciplined.

Take, for instance, Moses. Why did he die and not enter the Promised Land? It was over something simple: He struck the rock to find water instead of speaking to the rock. He did not listen to God's instruction (Num 20:8–12).

Take, for instance, Israel's defeat of Jericho. How did a little nation defeat that great city? They listened to the words of the Lord. Can you imagine getting an assignment in battle like this: "Go march around the city seven days in a row, on the seventh day, walk around it seven times, blow trumpets, and scream. If you do that, the city will be yours?" Yet they obeyed and the city was a victorious battle. Soon after that they were

---

30. Ibid., 61–62.

told not to take anything from the city for themselves (Josh 6:18–19). But a man named Achan stole some items and hid them under his tent. After the next battle against the smallest of cities when thirty-six men were killed, his sin was exposed and Joshua had his entire family stoned (Josh 7:22–26).

Is it important to listen to God? Certainly, Achan's sons and daughters would have thought it important. Certainly the loved ones of those men who were killed in battle because of Achan's failure to listen would have thought it important.

Next in the history of Israel was the time of the judges, one of the darkest times in the history of the nation; for they did not listen to the judges that God raised up. That meant pain and suffering as other nations attacked them (Judg 2:16–20). Eventually, Israel asked for a king to be like the other nations. They selected a man named Saul, who ultimately lost his kingship because he did not listen to God. Although he did so many things wrong, one of the turning points was when he did not completely wipe out the Amalekites as he was told to do (1 Sam 15:1–3). As Samuel confronted Saul, he said, "Because *you have rejected the word of the Lord*, He has also rejected you from being king" (1 Sam 15:23, emphasis mine).

David then became king and was mightily blessed by the Lord. In the story of David, God showed himself to be of extreme mercy and grace; for David failed to listen as well but did not get the punishments that Saul and Achan received. Why? The only explanation is that it was God's sovereign plan.

David's son, Solomon, failed to listen to God. He had one thousand wives and concubines who tore his heart away from God to serve other gods (1 Kgs 9:1–7). What did he get for his choice? The splitting of the nation of Israel.

The rest of the Old Testament tells the same story. Jeroboam, the first king in the divided kingdom for the northern region of Israel, had his hand withered right before his eyes and then healed. Still, he did not listen to the Lord (1 Kgs 13). Jonah failed to listen and had to spend three nights in the belly of a fish to wake up.

What about the New Testament? Does God take listening by his people as seriously now? Are we judged to the same degree as they were in the Old Testament, or were those just special phenomena? Al Mohler said, "As Christians, we live by the Word of God just as completely as Israel did."[31]

At the transfiguration, the Father made a very direct statement concerning the son: "This is My beloved Son, with whom I am well-pleased; listen to Him!" (Matt 17:5). Even in his first recorded sermon, Jesus said that the difference between a wise man and a foolish man is whether or not he hears his (Jesus') words and acts on them or not (Matt 7:24-27). This passage will be discussed at length in chapter 5. James said that individuals delude themselves if they do not obey God's word (Jas 1:22-25). The Apostle John said, "Blessed is he who reads and those who hear the words of the prophecy, and heed the things which are written in it; for the time is near" (Rev 1:3).

The point is that New Testament Christians have been continually told the same message that people in the Old Testament were told: They should listen and obey the truth of God's word. If they do, they will be blessed. Why are the results for not doing so less tragic than in the Old Testament? Only God knows that answer, but New Testament Christians should be thankful for his grace and mercy.

Preachers are to preach! Listeners are to listen! God still speaks through what he has spoken through his Holy Scriptures. As preachers and listeners work in harmony with each other, they can hear and understand the words of God. That is the preaching intersection, and that is where we all should want to be. We should want to hear God speak. We should desire to find ourselves at that intersection every time we set foot into a church and listen to a preacher preach God's word.

As listeners, we have little input into the preacher's side of the equation; but with the help of the Lord, we have everything to do with the listener's side. Starting in the next chapter, we will get very specific about the practical steps we can take as listeners to get the most out of the preaching of God's word. There are several keys that will help unlock our listening to the preaching of God's word. Keep reading and praying that God will make us the listeners he wants us to be.

---

31. Ibid., 63.

2

Receive the Preaching of God's Word

EVERYONE HAS EXPERIENCED IT. Everyone has had the busyness of a week; the craziness of Saturday evenings; and unexpected, almost comedic Sunday mornings. Everyone has experienced what Johnny and Sue recently went through:

> Sue woke up to the monotonous sound of her alarm and quickly realized, as she glanced at the clock, that she had snoozed a few too many times. She realized that they were late and were going to struggle to get to church on time. Sue woke Johnny up and told him to get breakfast going for their two children, Sammy (eight-year-old boy) and Allison (six-year-old girl). Johnny incoherently agreed. Sue quickly jumped out of bed and attempted to set a world record in what she knew was impossible: a fast shower. She was rushed, felt overwhelmed, and got out of the shower only to find Johnny still under the covers. "Johnny," she yelled, "we are late; you said you would get breakfast going."
>
> He rolled out of bed and said, "I just wanted five more minutes," which was actually more like fifteen. As he strolled to the kitchen to set the cereal and bowls out, he disgustingly yelled back, "What? Are you telling me that we have no milk?" And then he quickly remembered that he was supposed to pick it up the previous day when he was at the store and had forgotten. "What?" Sue replied. Johnny responded, "How about toasted waffles for breakfast?"
>
> After getting breakfast ready, Johnny set world records getting his shower. Sue stirred the children. It was amazing, she thought, that on days when nothing was going on they were up before the crack of dawn; but when there was school or something to do, it was like trying to wake up the dead. She yelled at them to wake up for the fifth time as Johnny walked out of the bathroom with toilet paper stuck all over his face. "I cut myself shaving again because I was rushed," he muttered.

They finally got the kids up, inhaled some food, and headed out the door to the garage only to realize that Sue had left the family van outside instead of putting it in the garage. "Why didn't you park it in the garage?" asked Johnny. "I can't believe you did this. Who is going to start the van now in this torrential rain storm?" Sue said, "I'll do it." But then Johnny felt a bit guilty and played the part of the victim, "No, I'm the man. I am supposed to do this."

The entire ten minutes to church nobody talked; but Sue was thinking of how she let her husband down and her children down and wondered if she would ever be a good wife or mother. She was feeling depressed and sad and hated what she had become. She was feeling a little bitter towards Johnny and the kids because they were making her late to her favorite part of church, the music.

Johnny was quiet as well, drifting between wondering if he could play this victim card (for having to go out in the rain to start the car) long enough to have nothing to do with the family after church because his favorite football team was playing their rivals. He was scheming and thinking and couldn't wait till church was over.

Finally, they arrived, not talking about anything that happened that morning. They rushed their kids to their classes and walked into the worship center (now almost ten minutes late), grabbed seats in the back, sang the remaining couple of songs, and took deep breaths as the pastor got up to preach.

What did the next forty-five minutes have in store for Johnny and Sue? Although for some reason this is humorous, how prepared were Johnny and Sue to hear from God in the sermon? Most likely, Sue was pondering what had happened and Johnny was focused on what was to happen after church so that probably nothing the pastor said was impactful upon either of their lives. Sure, they would leave feeling better about themselves and would even tell the preacher, "Good job," on the way out of church; but nothing had changed. It was just another Sunday morning among many others. The last thing on their minds was preparing for the sermon. They neglected the one thing they should have taken seriously, preparing themselves to listen to the preaching of God's word.

People live their lives preparing. For example, they prepare for vacations. Not many people decide to go on vacation, jump into the car, and start driving. They spend time making hotel reservations, looking at maps, booking airlines, and so on. People prepare for weddings. People prepare for Christmas and other holidays by decorating, baking goods, and buying presents. People even prepare for the weekly things of life, such as having company.

But what about preparing for church and the preaching of God's word? Of all the things that people plan, write in their calendars, and spend time on throughout the weeks and months, the most important thing that needs preparation is the one thing that is often overlooked: preparing for the sermon. Will it make a difference in individuals' lives if they prepare for the sermon the way they prepare for the normal activities of everyday life? Will it make a difference in their ability to listen to the sermons being preached?

What are the common problems that people have with preaching? I have heard things such as these: "It is boring." "It is too deep." "It is too shallow." "It does not deal with the real issues of life." "It does not address the personal issues that I am currently going through." "It is too long." "It is too short." "It is not organized and easy to follow." "It is too structured, like a commentary." Sound familiar? Can it be possible that the only real problem is that we come to sermons unprepared? That does not mean the other problems are not real issues, but can it be that those issues get our attention because we come to church ill prepared to listen?

The church located in the city of Thessalonica, started by the Apostle Paul, was prepared to hear from God's word. This church is really an example of what it means to be ready to listen to the word of God preached. Their church began after Paul entered their city and preached the gospel of Jesus Christ to them over the course of three Sabbaths (Acts 17:1–3).

A few years later, Paul wrote to them and recounted this event with them: "For this reason we also constantly thank God that *when you received the word of God* which you heard from us, you accepted it not as the word of men, but for what it really is, the word of God, which also performs its work in you who believe" (I Thess 2:13, emphasis mine). Paul said, reflecting on the event, that he was thankful because they had received the word of God, which means that they allowed the word of God to come alongside of them. They gave the word of God an audience, an attentive audience. They were ready to listen and hear from Paul as he preached. They listened to the word of God with interest.[1] This indicated that they had an active response to the message. They heard the words that came out of the apostle's mouth, and they sat under those words.

---

1. Mayhue, *First and Second Thessalonians*, 80.

They received the words, meaning they listened to what he had to say with some form of curiosity and some form of attentiveness.

In other words, they were prepared to listen to the sermon as Paul came and preached it. They did not take it for granted. There was awareness and alertness. They were not late, they were not tired, they were not inattentive, and they simply did not have an "I really don't care" attitude. They modeled what it means to come prepared for the preaching of God's word. When we come into church, do we come prepared to receive, to listen with interest to the message that is from the word of God?

Why is this important? Let me illustrate by volume. How many sermons will average Christians listen to in their lifetimes? Take for example the person who is forty years old. Assuming that this person started to listen to sermons at the age of ten years, this person has been a listener for thirty years. Now, let us assume that on average this person has attended a church that has two preaching times a week and has been a faithful attendee. That means this person has listened to 3,120 sermons. For how many of them did this average listener prepare to listen with interest? This is not a little issue, for by the time such persons get to the end of their lives, they will have sat through an astronomical number of sermons.

So how do we prepare for sermons? That is the question. The rest of this chapter is simply practical guidelines for *receiving* the word of God, for allowing the word of God to come alongside of us so that we can listen with interest. Proper listening will only be available when we prepare ourselves both physically and spiritually.

PREPARING PHYSICALLY

The preparation of the physical body has an impact upon how we listen to sermons on Sunday mornings. There is a little saying that has had so much impact on me and stands as an umbrella over what it means to prepare for the preaching from God's word: *Sunday mornings begin Saturday night*. When I was in high school, my youth pastor told us this all the time: If we want to have an effective Sunday morning, we must begin with preparations on Saturday night. To help visualize this concept, let us once again look into the lives of Johnny and Sue.

> Ten minutes into the sermon, Sue looked over and noticed that Johnny had started nodding to the preacher in the affirmative,

but his eyes were closed. Upon closer examination, Johnny was struggling, as always, to stay awake. As she gave him the elbow alarm clock, he almost jumped out of his seat. Now awake, he leaned over and said, "Why did you do that? I was just trying to concentrate on the sermon. I wasn't asleep." Knowing that those were just words, Sue wondered why her husband always had a problem staying awake for the sermon.

She remembered her pastor saying at one point that one of the keys to Sunday mornings is how you spend your Saturdays. She briefly replayed their "day off" yesterday in her mind. She remembered Johnny quickly jumped out of bed at 5:00 a.m. so that he could get to the golf course for his early tee time. He was home by 11:00 a.m., just in time to take their son, Sammy, to his basketball game—a double header, nonetheless. In the afternoon, Johnny made his best effort to mark off a few items from the "honey do" list that she had been saving for him. He finished just in time to head over to their friends' house for a quick dinner and game night. Around 9:00 p.m., they came home because they needed to get the kids into bed. Then Johnny started to watch a late game of college football. She imagined that he drifted off to sleep around midnight, if not later. Sue started to realize why she continued week after week to use her elbow on his ribs.

Sue then noticed that she had not heard a word the pastor had said in the last five minutes and made a mental effort to listen for the rest of the sermon. But maybe Sue thought, it would have been better if they had not even come, for what purpose was it serving?

Sound familiar? How many times have we thought that it was not even worth our time to be at church either because we were too tired or we had lots of things we needed to get done at the house? We think, "After all, we hardly get much out of the sermon anyway." Sometimes the body, when it is unprepared, gets in the way of the spirit and hinders it from learning wisdom and understanding. Yet there are ways we can prepare our bodies physically for preaching.

Come Rested

Have you ever fallen asleep during the sermon? Be honest. Odds are that you have closed your eyes only to open them to realize that time has passed. Has your spouse ever been relegated to using the elbow? Odds are he or she has. One of my sons is now seven years old and sits in the preaching service on Sunday nights with us. We still see a marked difference in him when he takes a nap on Sunday afternoons. I recall one time, when he did not take a nap, he really struggled staying awake. I remember looking over at him. His eyelids seemed to weigh over one hundred pounds. You know those cartoons in which people are so tired that they have to use toothpicks to hold their eyelids open? Well, that is exactly what our son looked like. We have all felt the weight of our own eyelids at some point during a sermon.

So why are people tired? Is it because the preacher is too boring? Is it because the preacher is too long? Is it because he is not doing a good enough job? Or is it because they have not come rested? There is a great passage in the book of Acts that many preachers use to justify the length of their sermons: "On the first day of the week, when we were gathered together to break bread, Paul began talking to them, intending to leave the next day, and he prolonged his message until midnight. There were many lamps in the upper room where we were gathered together. And there was a young man named Eutychus sitting on the window sill, sinking into a deep sleep; and as Paul kept on talking, he was overcome by sleep and fell down from the third floor and was picked up dead" (Acts 20:7–9).

Not many people can really imagine the preacher going so long that he goes past midnight. Some may even break into a sweat at the mere thought of it. Although preachers preaching from evening until midnight may be a good excuse for being tired and falling asleep, what sort of excuse can we use when they preach for thirty minutes? Forty-five minutes? Sixty minutes?

There are a couple of ways to come rested to sermons. First, get a good night's sleep. We should make sure to get as much sleep as we need to be productive. If we need eight hours of sleep every night to be fully productive, then we should get eight hours. If we only require five, then we should make sure to get five hours. We should plan ahead to make certain of plans so that we get a good night's sleep. Remember the motto: Sunday morning begins Saturday night.

It is okay to sleep. It is a necessary component of life. We have to sleep. In fact, one physician said this about our need for sleep: "A person can't do without sleep. He may keep it at bay for hours or even days, but eventually everyone must surrender to it. Sleep is indispensable to life itself. Sleep is good for us. It is so important, that even rest is no substitute for sleep . . . Sleep provides wakefulness, the alertness needed to be responsible. This one-third of life makes the other two-thirds possible. Even if the only function is to enable us to stay alert while awake, this function must be recognized, understood, and respected in our day-to-day lives."[2]

Yet while you get sleep, please remember that too much sleep can make a person lazy in life. Living in a state of laziness will make a person more tired: "Laziness casts into a deep sleep, and an idle man will suffer hunger" (Prov 19:15). This is a solemn reminder not to live our lives in a state of laziness because that laziness will simply produce more laziness. Doing nothing often makes us more tired. We may think that it is the opposite, that hard work will make us tired and bring about deep sleep; but this proverb makes it very clear that laziness in life will make a person sleepier. Just one chapter later in Proverbs, a stern warning is given to those who love to sleep: "Do not love sleep, or you will become poor; open your eyes, and you will be satisfied with food" (Prov 20:13). On the other hand, some people play so hard in life that they disrupt their normal schedules. Some people play so hard on Saturdays because it is their only day off from work that they are too tired on Sunday mornings.

Therefore, strive to be consistent with sleep. If we know that we have to get up early to get the kids up or to be at church early for something, then we may need to go to bed earlier that night. To come rested to the sermon, we must get a good night's sleep.

Another way to come rested is to get physical exercise. This is certainly something that many of us do not want to hear, but physical exercise will help. The Bible does talk about bodily discipline and exercising in 1 Timothy 4:7-8: "Discipline yourself for the purpose of godliness; for bodily discipline is only of little profit, but godliness is profitable for all things, since it holds promise for the present life and also for the life to come." Note what it says. Bodily discipline is only of little profit because compared to spiritual discipline, which has benefits not only for this life but also for the life to come, bodily discipline has benefits only for this life. It is easy to read that passage and think only the spiritual matters, not the physical at all; but it says that physical discipline does have some profit.

Many studies have shown that exercise has benefits beyond simply losing weight or staying fit. Some benefits of exercise can affect people who desire to listen well to sermons. Exercise can boost brainpower and give a person energy. According to one study,

2. Smith, *Medical Desk Reference*, 122.

> You might be surprised at how, say, popping in a workout tape for 30 minutes in the morning can change your whole day. When endorphins are released into your bloodstream during exercise . . . you feel much more energized the rest of the day. And when you improve your strength and stamina, it's easier to accomplish everyday tasks like carrying groceries and climbing stairs. This also helps you feel more energetic over the course of the day . . . While exercise may make you feel more tired at first . . . that won't last long. The physical tiredness you feel after working out isn't the same as everyday fatigue . . . Besides, once your body adjusts to exercise, you'll have more energy than ever.[3]

I know the first week or two after I began to work out I wanted to come home and go straight to bed. I complained that I had been sold a lie about exercise bringing more energy. But it comes eventually. The more I exercised the more energy I began to have.

If we really believe in biblical preaching, that it is the word of God opened and explained to give God's message for us, and if exercise makes us more alert, attentive, and restful, then we should get on that treadmill all to God's glory so we can hear him better through the preaching of his word. As we struggle with working out, we should think that the workout will help us listen to God better this week. Maybe the "little profit" that Paul talks about is the profit of keeping alert so that we can better discipline ourselves spiritually.

Coming rested helps both the person and the preacher. When those in the congregation are rested, they are more likely to interact with their preachers as they preach. They are more likely to laugh at their preachers' jokes. They may be more likely to nod their heads in affirmation when their preachers make good points. They may be more likely to verbally say "amen" in agreement to something that has touched their hearts. Communication (even nonverbal) can encourage, strengthen, and energize preachers. Friends, let us all come rested.

Come Filled

To come filled simply means that we come to church with our stomachs filled with food or drink so that we will not be thinking about the pot roast in the crock pot or the restaurant we will be making a mad

---

3. Sarnataro, "Top Ten Fitness Facts," lines 20–24.

dash towards after church. Our society hardly ever ignores the instinct to eat. When the stomach yells, we answer. And when it yells, it can be a distraction that keeps us from concentrating on what the preacher is talking about.

The people of Israel struggled with letting their physical needs of food and water distract them from obeying and listening to God when they were coming out of Egypt. Read about the Israelites' experience in Exodus 15–16 sometime. It is clear that while the people of Israel were wandering in the desert with Moses, they complained because they were starving and thirsty. Simply put, they allowed their physical conditions of hunger and thirst to dictate their thoughts. They were so completely focused on their stomachs that they took their focus off their Lord God and did so repeatedly. Yet when they were thirsty, the Lord provided water for them out of nowhere. When they were hungry, God caused birds to invade their camp or little wafers to appear on the ground. To be clear, the reason God provided the food and water to them was to make a point to them: He was their God. He wanted to show them that he had listened and that he had them right where he wanted them, not in Egypt eating the fat but dependent upon him. Once they received the food and water, they did well for a period of time but eventually focused on the physical food and water again.

When listeners of sermons become hungry, they lose focus as well. My kids often become hungry to the point that they are going to "die" if they do not eat soon. I know they are not going to die, but they think they are. They become so focused on their stomachs that no matter what I say to them, they only think of food.

Simply put, just do everything possible to take this distraction away. Everyone should come to church after following their normal routines. If we normally eat big breakfasts, then eat a big breakfast. If we are just bagel-and-coffee persons, then do that. If we eat nothing for breakfast normally, then maybe we can get away with it and not be distracted by our stomachs during the service. Whatever the body is used to having, provide it and prepare it to sit under the preaching of God's word.

The opposite is also true. Avoid eating too much. Eating too much can make a person tired and sick. Proverbs 25:16 says, "Have you found honey? Eat only what you need, that you not have it in excess and vomit it." We should avoid going to the local all-you-can-eat breakfast buffet in the morning before church, so that we do not have to sit in church with our stomachs in an uproar. Friends, let us all come filled.

Come Healthy

This does not mean that we should only come when we are healthy. It means we should live our lives to avoid getting sick. We should avoid situations and things that are going to produce illness that will keep us from coming to church and being under the preaching of God's word.

Are there any motivations for staying healthy? Recently I asked a group of people this question. Some of them wanted to stay healthy because they simply felt better. Nobody likes being sick. Some said that it just made life more enjoyable. Others wanted to stay healthy so they could do more playing in life. Other responses included to be more productive in work, to increase their attractiveness or appearance, to live longer, and to keep those medical bills lower. Then I asked them this question: "What about maintaining good health so that we can be better prepared to listen to the preaching of God's word?" This is something that most people never really think about as a motivation.

The Bible says that caring for the body pleases the Lord. The Apostle Paul said that the body does not belong to the Christian but is the temple of God (I Cor 3:16–17; 6:19–20). According to Smith, "Taking good care of the body, then, is proper STEWARDSHIP of the temple of the Holy Spirit. A Christian should go to the doctor not primarily to get well, but to be a good steward. One takes his car to the tire repair shop to fix a flat tire so as to be able to use the car in the most efficient manner. Likewise, one takes his body to the doctor so that he will be able to use it for the Lord with maximum efficiency . . . Maintaining good health is for the purpose of glorifying God."[4]

The goal should be to maintain as best we can healthy lives, realizing that even our best efforts do not guarantee healthy lives. Illness is a result of sin entering into the world. Sometimes situations occur in life when we are unable to hear the preaching from God's word because of some sort of physical affliction that is outside of our control. However, we need to strive for this to be the exception, not the rule.

So how do we do it? How do we maintain healthy lives? One of the first things that we can do is to consult our doctors. That probably

---

4. Smith, *Medical Desk Reference*, 5.

means yearly physicals. As indicated in the previous quote, we do many preventative things in our lives. We do preventative work on our cars (oil changes and tune ups); we do preventative work on our lawn machines (change oils, spark plugs, service, and blade sharpening); we do preventative work on our houses (painting and filter changing). So why not take preventative action in caring for our bodies, the only thing that is said to be a temple of God?

There are other things to do as well. Maybe it means exercise, which was mentioned under the second point. Maybe it means eating healthier, getting vitamins that our bodies so desperately need. Maybe it means not drinking as much coffee or soda, getting off the caffeine and drinking enough water for our bodies. Maybe it means not filling ourselves with junk food all the time. We should learn to become students of our own bodies.

The most disciplined person I ever read about is Jonathan Edwards, a puritan pastor who lived from 1703 to 1758. Before he was twenty years old, Edwards wrote seventy resolutions that would govern his life to ensure that his entire life came under the Lordship of Christ. His twentieth resolution says, "Resolved, to maintain the strictest temperance in eating and drinking."[5] He was so disciplined and concerned about what went in his body that when he was twenty-one years old, he wrote this in his diary: "By a sparingness in diet, and eating as much as may be what is light and easy of digestion, I shall doubtless be able to think more clearly, and shall gain time; 1. By lengthening out my life; 2. Shall need less time for digestion, after meals; 3. Shall be able to study more closely, without injury to my health; 4. Shall need less time for sleep; 5. Shall more seldom be troubled with the head-ache."[6] He modeled and taught us that we should know what is good and what is not good for our bodies. This will motivate us to do things that will help us prepare to listen to the preaching of God's word.

There is one more question that needs to be asked in this regard: Do we have the same standard of illness when it comes to work and church? Do we go to work when we are sick because we have no more sick days and may possibly lose pay but not go to church because, well, we simply do not have to be there? The point is to place as high a standard on church as on work. We should avoid that temptation to think, "I will

5. Nichols, *Jonathan Edwards'*, 19.
6. Edwards, *The Works of Jonathan Edwards*, lxxvii.

just get the CD or listen to the sermon on the Internet." That is good and should be done if we are unable to be at church, but it is not the same. There is something special about being at a live preaching event.

If we are sick and do come to church, we should come prepared. Bring tissues, bring cough drops, bring the things you will need while sitting there to make it easier to listen to the sermon. Friends, let us all come healthy.

Come Focused

Jay Adams, in his book *Be Careful How You Listen*, quoted the church father John Chrysostom on the problem of distractions in the service. These words should pierce every heart: "Please listen to me—you are not paying attention. I am talking to you about the Holy Scriptures, and you are looking at the lamps and the people lighting them. It is very frivolous to be more interested in what the lamplighters are doing . . . After all, I am lighting a lamp too—the lamp of God's Word."[7]

How easy it is for us to become so engaged in other things rather than the preacher! We are so easily distracted from the preaching of God's word. When the preacher stands up to preach, lock in on him, focus on him, and tune out all other things except the preacher and his voice. Our focus should be like that of those participants in the synagogue in Nazareth early in Jesus' ministry.

There is a wonderful account recorded for us in Luke's gospel about how those people focused on the preacher that day:

> And He came to Nazareth, where He had been brought up; and as was His custom, He entered the synagogue on the Sabbath, and stood up to read. And the book of the prophet Isaiah was handed to Him. And He opened the book and found the place where it was written, "THE SPIRIT OF THE LORD IS UPON ME, BECAUSE HE ANOINTED ME TO PREACH THE GOSPEL TO THE POOR. HE HAS SENT ME TO PROCLAIM RELEASE TO THE CAPTIVES, AND RECOVERY OF SIGHT TO THE BLIND, TO SET FREE THOSE WHO ARE OPPRESSED, TO PROCLAIM THE FAVORABLE YEAR OF THE LORD." And He closed the book, gave it back to the attendant and sat down; and *the eyes of all in the synagogue were fixed on Him*. (Luke 4:16–20, emphasis mine)

---

7. Adams, *Be Careful*, 81.

All Jesus did was open the word of God, read from it, and then sit back down. Yet everyone's eyes were fixed on him. That means they were completely focused on him, all of their eyes were on him, looking intently at him, waiting for what he had to say next. He had their attention!

Contrast the people of Nazareth with Johnny and Sue.

> Sue had done a good job of listening for a few minutes when she was distracted by the cough of someone further down her aisle. She quickly glanced to notice that Betty was struggling with a little cold. While noticing her cold, Sue also saw that Betty had had her hair cut this past week. "I wonder where she goes to get her hair cut; it looks so cute on her," she thought. Then she remembered that it was time for her to make an appointment for Allison (her daughter) and her to get their hair cut. "I have to ask her after the service where she went. I need to find a new hairdresser."
>
> As she attempted to tune back into the preacher, someone walked past her. She assumed the person had to use the restroom. She wondered why people always left the service but then realized that she sort of had to use the restroom as well. She was determined to wait until after the service. All of a sudden, she noticed everyone around her turning their Bibles to a new portion of Scripture, but she had no idea where they were turning. She tried to listen for a few moments to get a clue about where to turn. Then the kids sitting in front of her turned around with their Sunday school suckers in their mouths. Seeing that food almost made her stop breathing. "Oh, no," she thought, "I forgot to set the oven time bake. The casserole for lunch is not going to bake. What are we going to eat for lunch? I guess we could have leftovers, but I know how much Johnny doesn't like that. I'm just not sure what to have for lunch."
>
> As she sat there thinking about lunch, she realized that Johnny needed another elbow. She leaned over to him. "Pay attention. This is church. You should be listening to the preacher." As the words came out of her mouth, she realized that although not sleeping, she too had certainly been distracted from the sermon.

A little too familiar isn't it? There were things that distracted them, that caused them not to focus on the preacher like the people in Nazareth were fixed on Jesus. There are a few distractions that everyone should seek to avoid.

First, avoid the bathroom distraction. Is it really too simple to say this, go before church. Use the facilities before entering the worship center, before the singing of songs, before the preaching of the word of God. If adults have children with them in the service, make them go before as well. Set down some rules that they are not allowed to leave the service to use the bathroom. I am shocked at how many parents let their children leave during the service.

Leaving during the service to use the bathroom (or really for any reason) is a major distraction to three groups of people. First, it distracts you. You miss part of the word from God. Think about it: When the preacher stands up and opens the word of God and explains it, it is God's message for you. In most instances, leaving to use the bathroom can wait until after God's special word is given to you. Imagine the president of the United States is coming to your place of business and giving one speech. He will only be there for forty-five minutes. He is in the middle of the speech and you realize that you have to use the facilities. Will you waste this opportunity or do everything you can to hold it? Although this may be a dumb illustration, it proves the point. In most cases, however, we do not hold it because we do not see the sermon as being that important.

Second, it distracts others. When we get up to leave during the service, we may unwittingly cause others to be distracted from the word that God has for them. Just like those around Sue, we can disrupt others from hearing from God.

Third, it distracts the preacher. The preacher has probably spent a majority of his week studying and praying that the truth he learned will have an impact on his people. Yet we have a habit of leaving. What is he thinking as he is preaching when he sees people leaving? "Aren't they getting it?" "Am I not communicating it well enough?" "Am I being boring?" It not only distracts him but also discourages him. One of the greatest ways we can encourage our preachers is by being there and not leaving.

Second, avoid the people distraction. What Sue went through epitomizes everyone. We see other people and then think of them and what is going on in their lives. We notice what they are wearing, how they've styled their hair, and who they are sitting by; or we think of their children and of setting up a play date for the kids. It is easy to think of anything but the sermon.

Being distracted by people is counterproductive to the purpose of being at church. We go to church to encourage one another to spiritual growth, to fellowship, to love. There will be plenty of time to think about other people. When the preacher gets up behind that pulpit and opens God's word, it should be just him and us; it should be just God and us!

What are we to do? Sit in the front rows, the cheap seats in the worship center. Some people do not even know that they exist, but there are seats towards the front of the worship center that are usually unoccupied. Sitting towards the front of the church will help ensure that when people get up and leave the service, we are not distracted. Plus, it will encourage the preacher.

At the same time, avoid being the person that distracts others. The Bible makes it clear that there are some people who come to church with the intent of being noticed by others. In the church pastored by Timothy, this was a big problem. There were women who were getting all dressed up to come to church, hoping to have all the attention on them. It was to these women that Paul gave some very direct instruction on the heart attitude of coming to church (1 Tim 2:9–10). According to his instruction, we should never come to church with the intent of being the one noticed. God wants us to check our motives for coming to worship at church. Is it something about us or all about him?

Third, avoid the distraction of random thoughts. It is helpful to avoid this third distraction if we are going to get the most out of the sermon. The human mind is amazing but has the tendency to wander. I often tell people that I cannot think of anything until I have to think of only one thing. Here is a test. Don't think of an elephant! What did you just think of? An elephant? Just hearing something makes the mind wander, pondering something other than what we desire to concentrate on.

The best example of a wandering mind in my own life happens when I spend longer times in prayer. Spending time praying requires discipline to focus on my prayers. The longer I pray, the more I think of all the things that I needed to do during the past week that did not get done. I think of sermon illustrations. I think of old friends I have not seen in years. I think of what the future will be like. I think of my children and of what they are doing. Sometimes I have to stop and ask myself, "Have I even prayed about anything that I wanted to pray about?" Has that ever happened to you? It has probably also happened in church, right? Well, what can we do about it?

The most effective thing we can do is to keep a pad of note paper close by and simply jot these thoughts down. We focus on these thoughts because we fear we will forget them later. By just writing them down quickly, we can come back to them after the sermon. Make it a habit that once a thought is on paper, it is no longer in your mind.

Even as I write this, I am on my fifth day of having no power due to an ice storm and several inches of snow. My basement is flooded, and my children are complaining that it is too cold inside the house. It has been a horrible week. While I am trying to concentrate on writing and studying, all these thoughts are going through my head to distract me. It is something that I must fight against in the same way we must fight against distracting thoughts during sermons. As a famous idiom says, "Practice makes perfect." The more we work at focusing and avoiding random thoughts or dwelling on random thoughts, the more likely we will be successful at avoiding this distraction.

Fourth, avoid the distractions of children. The easiest way to avoid these distractions is to use the resources the church provides. If there is a nursery, take advantage of it. If there are other children's ministries, such as Sunday school or children's church, or other things for children during the worship service, take advantage of them. Those classes should be designed to teach children the Bible at age-appropriate levels for them.

The big question is always, however, at what age should they be in the service to sit under the preaching of God's word. Jay Adams made some good points in regards to this:

> If you refuse your children admittance to the preaching service until such a time as they are old enough to understand the message (no set age is given: some children mature before others), they will not develop poor listening habits, which become ingrained over the years. Moreover, they will not distract others (including their parents) by antics on the pews, or by running to the bathroom. And, perhaps of greatest importance, they will be anxious to "graduate" to that advanced stage where they are allowed to come to the preaching service. They will consider listening a privilege rather than a punishment![8]

A few highlights are needed. Having children in the service before they are able to understand the preacher can result in their developing poor habits that will be really difficult to overcome later in life. I think

---

8. Ibid., 87.

about my own children now. On Sunday nights, they are in the service with us. They do a really good job of sitting still. But I think they often check out of reality and sit there brain dead. I wonder if they are developing habits right now that are going to be hard to break: habits of not actively listening, habits of not paying attention, habits of day dreaming, habits that do not help with their listening to preaching.

One argument against using the services the church has to offer is that the parents need to be the spiritual leaders and teach their children how to listen to sermons. This is true, but what are parents teaching their children about listening to sermons when they are distracted and walk out of the sermons with nothing to apply to their lives? In addition, the most important part of teaching children spiritually is everyday life, not just the sermon (Deut 6:4–9). The training of children should be done through all of life: at the grocery store, at the local YMCA as they play sports, at school as they interact with their friends, at home as they go to bed. People who think their only parenting responsibility is teaching their children how to listen to sermons during the worship service are doing a disservice to their children and are probably not being very effective.

Another argument is that people want to teach their kids the discipline to sit still. But can't they learn the art of sitting still at home while not developing poor habits that they will fight to change when they are older? Aren't there many other opportunities to teach young children to sit still?

Concerning children in the worship service, I often think of my precious wife. I tend to think that our children do a fairly good job of sitting still. However, they can still be distracting. One child is leaning on her, one is asking for paper and pen, then one grabs the hymnal and thumbs through it, and so the entire service goes. There are some Sunday nights I am surprised when she walks out of the service that she has heard anything the preacher said.

At what age should children be in the worship service? I have intentionally avoided the answer to this question, for the Scriptures do not speak of the age at which a child is ready to sit under the preaching of God's word. It gives principles that need application. Ultimately it is up to the individual parent's discretion. Certainly it depends upon the growth of the child. At some point, if they are old enough to sit still, listen, and get something out of someone talking at school for long periods of time, then they should be old enough to sit through sermons, listen effectively, and be able to learn. It also may depend on the preacher. If the preacher is more content driven, then it will be more difficult for the child to learn. But if the preacher is more application or persuasively driven, then it may be easier for children to learn at an earlier age. All parents should think of their children, know their children, and not rely upon a certain magic age at which their children are now ready when the day before they were not.

The adults must take seriously the moment children begin to sit in the service. Spend time after church with them talking about the sermon to reinforce the importance of what just happened. In addition, parents need to be very aware of leading others into distractions because of their children. They need to be sensitive to others. If their children are crying or are out of control, they need to think of those sitting around them.

These distractions are just the tip of the iceberg. We know what distracts us more than others, so we need to do everything we can to avoid those things. As Chrysostom was quoted earlier, we need to realize that the preacher is lighting the light of God's Word. That is more important than anything else that is going on in the service. Friends, let us all come focused.

Come Regularly

This should go without saying; but it is really hard to come rested, filled, healthy, and focused if we do not come at all. Church should not be an option for the person who claims the name of Jesus. For some people, the sermon is secondary to many other things, making it is easy to skip church. Imagine people who took church lightly in Thessalonica when Paul came to town. What if they were at the lake for a few weeks in the summer when Paul came? What if they were not feeling their best and missed the couple of weeks that Paul was the visiting preacher? What if they had gone on a little vacation to Corinth and decided to extend their trip a bit, even though they could have come back sooner? What if they had missed Paul's preaching? What if we miss our pastors' sermons this week? Will we think, "Oh, well, just another sermon?" Or will we think, "I have missed God's word for me this week." We need to condition our thinking to come regularly to the preaching of God's word.

As stated in the first chapter, God still speaks through that which he has written. When the preacher stands up and re-oralizes the word of God, it is as if God is audibly speaking. The preaching of God's word should take primacy. The pattern throughout the Old Testament and New Testament is that preaching, the proclamation of God's word, should be a priority.

In Hebrews, we are encouraged to "consider how to stimulate one another to love and good deeds, not forsaking our own assembling together, as is the habit of some, but encouraging one another; and all the more as you see the day drawing near" (Heb 10:24–25). The early church is said to have been "continually devoting themselves to the apostles' teaching and to fellowship, to the breaking of bread and to prayer" (Acts 2:42). They gathered daily—not weekly, not every other week, but daily! It is so easy for us to be far removed from that thinking. Attendance is one of the first signs of what is important in someone's heart.

What does it mean to come regularly? It means that we make every effort to make sure we are at the services that our churches provide, starting with the main worship service. We should plan our schedules so that we are at church. It means, as was mentioned earlier, that we come when we are sick, as long as we are not contagious. It means we have a high standard of attendance to come and listen to the preaching of God's word.

What about vacations? Are they vacations from work or vacations from church as well? There is something about getting out of town that makes us think we can miss church when Sunday rolls around. If we have to miss attending our churches during vacations, we should find churches that preach the Bible in the areas where we are vacationing and go there on Sunday morning.

If we attend churches in which the preacher's preaching is expositional in nature (verse by verse), the more we miss, the harder it is to understand the flow of the passages when we do attend. The texts of Scripture were written in a logical flow, and these pastors are attempting to show that flow. The more we miss, the harder we must work to pay attention.

One thing that may help with this is to make every effort never to be gone two weeks in a row. We should be diligent with our church attendance. Sit down at the beginning of the year and decide on an acceptable number of Sundays to miss during the year, scheduling vacations and time away so that only one Sunday is involved each time. Avoid hobbies that will take us away from church. Recently, I missed six straight Sunday mornings at my church. That's right, six! I spent a couple of weeks teaching in Russia and then spent four weeks helping a church through a transition. I missed my pastor preaching through the book of Third John. I missed it all. Friends, let us all come regularly.

Come Thoughtfully

We should come to church prepared with the things that we will need. This certainly means that we need to bring our Bibles. We may forget a lot of things, but we should never forget our Bibles. If we can go to church and never use the Bible, then maybe we need to find another church. The Bible should be the only source of authority that any pastor has. In Thessalonica, Paul reasoned from the Scriptures with the people. He taught them the word of God, not the word of Paul. Pastors need to preach the word, not themselves. As they should be faithful to do that, so should we be faithful to bring our Bibles in preparation for it.

When our pastors say to flip to certain references, we should flip to those references. We should look at the text. It may sound funny or strange, but the sound of pages turning is one of the most important sounds to preachers. It means that we are following them; it means that we are interested; it means that we care about what the word is going to say. It is one of the most encouraging things anyone can do to help preachers.

There is something special about looking in the text of God's word. The Bible is so special that men such as William Tyndale and Martin Luther made it their desire to translate the Bible into their native tongues because they knew the people needed to have the word of God in their own languages. I wonder whether the reason people do not bring their Bibles to church on Sunday is because it does not mean anything to them the rest of the week. J. C. Ryle addressed that thought:

> I fear we are in danger of forgetting that to have the Bible is one thing, and to read it quite another . . . In one house it lies in a corner, stiff, cold, glossy, and fresh as it was when it came from the bookseller's shop. In another it lies on a table, with its owner's name written in it—a silent witness against him day after day. In another it lies on some high shelf, neglected and dusty, to be brought down only on grand occasions, such as a birth in the family, like a heathen idol at its yearly festival. In another it lies deep down at the bottom of some box or drawer, among the things not wanted, and is never dragged forth into the light of day, until the arrival of sickness, the doctor, and death. Ah! These things are sad and solemn. But they are true.[9]

---

9. Ryle, *How Readest Thou*, 33–34.

Coming thoughtfully means we bring our Bibles, but it also means that we bring pen and paper to take notes. Ladies should not be rustling through their purses as preachers are giving their introductions, looking for pens buried at the bottom of priceless valuables. Have pens ready to be used. Know where they are. Friends, let us all come prepared.

PREPARING SPIRITUALLY

All of the advice I have mentioned so far are principles that can be applied by anyone going to weekly board meetings, sales meetings, employee meetings, or any local PTO or social speeches. But sermon events are more than just physical presentations of facts. There is something spiritual going on behind the scenes. We can do everything previously mentioned in the physical realm and still be poor listeners to sermons. Unless we work at preparing ourselves spiritually, we have little hope of being effective listeners to sermons.

The Apostle Paul made the connection of the battle between the physical and the spiritual when he said that "our struggle is not against flesh and blood, but against the rulers, against the powers, against the world forces of this darkness, against the spiritual forces of wickedness in the heavenly places" (Eph 6:12). The battle ultimately is not the fact that we stay up too late Saturday night and are tired on Sunday morning. Sure, there are little things we can do to take the physical distractions away from us; but the battle of being effective listeners to sermons is ultimately a spiritual battle. George Whitefield, one of the greatest preachers in the history of the church, had this to say concerning the preaching event: "Give diligent heed to the things that are spoken from the Word of God. If an earthly king was to issue out a royal proclamation, on performing or not performing the conditions therein contained, the life or death of his subjects entirely depended, how solicitous would they be to hear what those conditions were? And shall we not pay the same respect to the King of kings, and Lord of lords, and lend an attentive ear to his ministers, when they are declaring, in his name, how our pardon, peace, and happiness may be secured?"[10]

Because we are listening to a spiritual message, we should be attentive. That is what the rest of this chapter is about: preparing spiritually to listen to a spiritual message.

---

10. Whitefield, "Sermon 28," lines 67–71.

Come Hungry

Although we should come filled with physical food, we should come hungry for spiritual food, which means we should have a desire and passion for God's word. Christians are called to hunger for God's word. The Apostle Peter said, "Like newborn babies, long for the pure milk of the word, so that by it you may grow in respect to salvation" (1 Pet 2:2). Christians are commanded to long for the Bible. Not many Americans understand longing for something; if they want something, they get it. Not many people go for a day or two days without eating. If they do, their stomachs start to growl and they become irritated. Soon they are only focused on that one thing. The illustration Peter used is that of an infant who longs for or desires milk. We are to long for the word of God, which means that when we do not spend time in it and feed our spiritual souls, our spiritual stomachs start to growl. The twist is that once the physical has been satisfied, the craving is gone. However, the spiritual can never be satisfied; the cravings become stronger and stronger for more and more of the word.

The Scriptures are filled with people who hungered for the milk of the word. Job in the Old Testament said, "I have not departed from the command of his lips; I have treasured the words of his mouth more than my daily bread" (Job 23:12). Job said that even more important than the food that he needed to survive in this life was the word of God in his spiritual life. One of the greatest chapters in the Bible is Psalm 119 in which the author showed obvious hunger for the word of God: "I delight in your decrees; I will not neglect your word . . . Your statutes are my delight; they are my counselors . . . The law from your mouth is more precious to me than thousands of pieces of silver and gold" (vv. 16, 24, 72). More than a thousand pieces of silver or gold? Now that is hunger. That is passion. That is desire for God's word. How many of us can really make that statement with integrity in our hearts? My guess is not many.

When Peter said in 1 Peter 2 that the Christian should "long" for the word of God, he used it in comparison to the cravings that characterize unbelievers. In 1 Peter 1:14, he said, "As obedient children, do not be conformed to the former lusts which were yours in your ignorance." Then in 1 Peter 2:11, he said, "Beloved, I urge you as aliens and strangers to abstain from fleshly lusts which wage war against your soul." In other words, Peter told them that before they were saved, they gave in to evil desires but now that they are saved, those things should not represent them. He reminded them that they were not members of this world and that the desires they had for the things of this world would only kill them. That means that in contrast to those things that unbelievers may crave, believers should crave spiritual things such as the word of God.

If there is anything that does *not* characterize the contemporary church, anything that does *not* capture the spirit of the so-called evangelicalism of the twenty-first century, it is pervasive, widespread love, hunger, and delight in the word of God. Why should people want to hunger or long for the word of God? The reason is that the Scriptures contain the spiritual food that their souls have been longing for their entire lives. We hunger for that which gives and contains the spiritual food that our souls ultimately desire.

It is possible at this point that someone may be wondering why this is important. John MacArthur, at the dedication of his study Bible, preached a sermon entitled "Cultivating a Hunger for God's Word":

> Now, when I was thinking about how I might want to present this very important Bible to you today and put it in your hands and with what scripture I might embrace this special moment, I was drawn to this passage immediately, because no matter what else I might have said, this is the most compelling issue at hand. It does no good to provide a tool like this if a person doesn't have a desire to study the word of God. If a person doesn't have a craving and a longing, then all of the notes, with all of the material that they provide, are really useless, unless there is a passion in the heart of the individual to read with understanding the scriptures. And so, we have to go back to the very foundation, which is to face the issue of whether or not we have such a craving. Nothing obviously would be sadder than to have all of this information explaining the meaning of scripture and have it stuck on a shelf somewhere.[11]

The same principles of application that MacArthur used in the study Bible are appropriate for sermons. The most compelling issue at hand is that it will do us no good to take notes, to go to bed early, to sit up front, to have the greatest system of note filing, or to avoid all distractions if we have no desire or hunger for the Word of God. Showing up at church is one thing, but having that burning passion within us that longs for God's word is quite another. We can all put on faces of passion that do not truly reflect our hearts. We need to develop in our hearts the

---

11. MacArthur, "Cultivating a Hunger for God's Word," lines 52–57.

same attitude Jeremiah had when he said, "Your words were found and I ate them, and Your words became for me a joy and the delight of my heart" (Jer 15:16).

How do we develop such a hungering? It starts today. It starts with discipline and planning. It starts with priorities. It starts with saying that even when we do not desire God's word, the only thing that is going to kindle that desire is spending time in God's word. The more time we spend in it, the more we will begin to hunger for it. It starts with the hard work of opening the Scriptures and reading God's word daily.

Maybe this metaphor will help bring this thought together. Sometimes people come to preaching events and treat them like broccoli. I have nothing against broccoli per se, but it just does not taste very good. My guess is that even people who eat broccoli probably do not long for it or hunger after it. As for myself, I do not want it. I am not interested in it. I do not want to smell it. I do not want it near any of my other food. Some may agree up to a point but say that broccoli is actually okay as long as it comes with cheese sauce. You see, sometimes people come to sermon events picky. Because they are not hungry, they simply pass by those foods that they do not like to eat. Even though I am a picky eater, I suppose there may be some scenario in which I will eat broccoli (a deserted island nightmare comes to mind). Even the pickiest of eaters will eat anything when they are hungry enough. That means that we live by this principle: The hungrier I am, the less picky I become.

Remember Paul warning Timothy that the time will eventually come when people will only want to listen to teachers who tickle their ears and only teach them things they want to hear (2 Tim 4:1–4)? Can it be that those who eventually run and turn do so because they come picky to the sermon table? Over time, they try to dictate what they need to hear based on what they like instead of on what God wants for them. Can it be that they do this because they are never really hungry for the word of God? They have never thirsted after God, which has spun out of control and become picking and choosing what they want to hear. Certainly some sermons will be like steaks and some like little pieces of vegetables; but if we come hungry, we will eat no matter what is served, as long as it is food from the word of God. Why? Because we know that the food we eat will have sustenance for our spiritual, eternal lives. The problem is not that we become full on the preaching, it is that we are not hungry enough for the table of God's word. Friends, let us all come hungry.

Come Worshipping

How passionate are we in worshipping God? How have we done in our personal worship of God during the last week? How are we doing at living up to the command given by the Apostle Paul when he said: "Therefore I urge you, brethren, by the mercies of God, *to present your bodies a living and holy sacrifice, acceptable to God, which is your spiritual service of worship*. And do not be conformed to this world, but be transformed by the renewing of your mind, so that you may prove what the will of God is, that which is good and acceptable and perfect" (Rom 12:1-2, emphasis mine).

There certainly are physical hang-ups that happen in getting ready for Sunday mornings, but what about the spiritual ones? Once again, let us learn from the life of Johnny and Sue.

> As Johnny and Sue sat in church, they actually heard something the pastor said and began to think about it. The pastor had just talked about giving your life so as to worship Jesus, only Jesus, every minute of every day. Sue looked over and realized that Johnny was finally paying attention; at least he appeared to be. She thought, "I have not done a good job this last week of worshiping Jesus every day." She thought about her attitude toward her husband and kids during the past week. She had not put them first in anything but had been selfish. She thought of how many little quirky things Johnny did that disgusted her. She thought of those words he said five years ago, still feeling hurt and resentment toward him. "I just can't forgive him," she thought.
>
> She remembered that at the local PTO meeting this last week she had been very unkind to some of the other women there and realized that she had not worshipped Jesus in those relationships. Then it dawned on her that Johnny still did not know about that credit card she had been hiding from him. She lied to her husband, rationalizing it by telling herself that there were so many people that did the same thing. She knew that she had not spent any time with God this week in his word and had hardly prayed at all. "I need to get into a Bible study or something," she thought but was afraid to talk to anyone for fear that they might ask her questions about her life. She did not want to answer any of them. Plus, they would not understand her weakness. It was better to keep it deep inside, even though she felt all alone. She decided to try just to do better this week, but somehow she knew she wouldn't.

Johnny was actually having similar thoughts as he reflected upon his week. He was feeling some guilt over the money he stole this past week at his office. It was just petty cash, and he planned on paying it back; but he knew deep down inside that he would not. He knew that he needed to get this problem taken care of but wondered if he ever would. He thought, "I just need to ignore it for a while and the guilt will at least go away. If that was the only problem, then I would tackle it, but there are so many things that have kept me from worshiping Jesus this week." He guessed he could probably locate his Bible if he had to, but what was the point. He thought of how he despised his wife over their intimacy or lack thereof. He knew that his new secretary at the office had been flirting with him, and somehow he knew that it would be wrong, but he liked the fact that she paid attention to him. He understood what the pastor said, but how could anyone worship Jesus all the time. That was an unrealistic standard.

As they both sat there, the rest of the pastor's sermon went over their heads, not because of the children in front of them or their tiredness but because of the spiritual issues in their hearts. Somehow they both realized that they needed to be there, but they were completely unprepared really to hear what their pastor was saying. They sort of caught each other's eyes, and they both knew it. It did not need to be said. They knew that they both could not wait until the sermon was over and they could get home. They resented who they were and had little hope of change.

Not quite as funny as before, is it? What were our stories for this past week? This past month? Was God part of them? Did we worship Jesus Christ this week? What are our plans for worshipping him tomorrow? We often think that even though the worship of Jesus is far from our thoughts all week, we can just show up at church, straighten our ties, and say, "Okay, let's worship God. Let's listen to the sermon. Let's do church and then go home to the persons we were before."

But worshipping God is not a light switch. It is not something that is just turned on at the appropriate time and then turned off when we are finished. Worshipping God is a 24/7 calling. It is not something that happens just at church buildings or just when the music starts or even just as preachers get up to preach. A. W. Tozer said, "If you cannot worship the Lord in the midst of your responsibilities on Monday, it is not very likely that you were worshiping on Sunday! Actually, none of us has the ability to fool God. Therefore, if we are so engaged in our Saturday pursuits that we are far from His presence and far from a sense of worship on Saturday, we are not in very good shape to worship Him on Sunday."[12]

Tozer is hard core, saying that the Christian should go to school or work tomorrow and think, "I need to worship God here today. The way I talk, what I listen to, the things I watch, the attitudes I have—they all are a part of my worship of God." They all play a part in preparing ourselves spiritually to have hearts of worship. Remember that umbrella statement: Sunday mornings begin Saturday nights. Honestly, Sunday morning should be the culmination of an entire week of preparation. We should be walking into church ready to worship.

This is exactly what the parable of the sower is teaching, that the preparation of the heart is important. Most church goers know the story chronicled in Mark 4 in which the sower sowed the seed (the word of God). Some of it fell on hard soil, some on rocky soil, some on thorny soil, and some on soft soil. Ultimately, Christ's point here is that the word of God only has long-lasting, penetrating results in those hearts that are soft. I think Christ is telling everyone about the different kinds of people who respond to the gospel, how they hear the word of God. This passage says something about what it means to approach the word of God and listen to it. At the end of the parable, Jesus gave a statement of warning: "He who has ears to hear, let him hear." (v. 9). Then a few verses later in the next parable (v. 24), Jesus said, "Take care what you listen to." There is strong evidence that these parables should be taken together as one big parable on how people listen, how they prepare themselves, and how they hear the word of God.

Do we come to sermons worshipping with stony hearts, rocky hearts, thorny hearts, or soft hearts? It is a good question because at every biblical sermon, the audience is placed at a crossroads. The one who comes worshipping is the one who has the soft heart. To be clear, in the parable, Jesus said that only one of those four are regenerate believers. Only those with the good soil are those who are really saved. They are the only ones who bring forth long-lasting fruit. Yet here is the reality: Even those with hearts of good soil can have bad times in their lives. They sometimes come to sermons or preaching events and listen like those with the other unregenerate soils. There are times when we come to church and our hearts are distracted spiritually, either through per-

12. Tozer, *Whatever Happened*, 122.

secution or the temptations of the world. Maybe there are times when we really do not care; we hope not many times, but in reality it does happen. We hope our hearts are mostly soft, fruit-bearing hearts. The admonition Jesus gave should be taken seriously: "Be careful how you listen" (Mark 4:24).

How do we come worshipping? *First, we must engage in the spiritual disciplines.* We must make certain we are reading our Bibles and praying every day. We should also make certain we are meditating and memorizing Scripture. There are many good books concerning spiritual disciplines. Pick one up and read it. As always, keep God's word central; there are no shortcuts to worshipping Christ. One word of advice when it comes to the spiritual disciplines in connection with sermons: Many people do great jobs of reading their Bibles and praying and walking with Christ during the week except for Sundays. It is almost as if people think because they are going to church, they can take the day off from personal Bible reading. If we usually get up in the morning and spend time with Jesus in his word, then we should do that on Sunday morning as well.

Second, we should seek to live lives of purity and holiness. We need to learn to say no to sin in our lives and learn to say yes to Christ. Do we grasp what Paul said in 1 Corinthians 10:13? "No temptation has overtaken you but such as is common to man; and God is faithful, who will not allow you to be tempted beyond what you are able, but with the temptation will provide the way of escape also, so that you will be able to endure it." We should be constantly looking for that way of escape. We should become spiritual Houdini's. We should develop lives of repentance and realize that we cannot do it ourselves.

Third, we should learn to sing good, theological, soul-stirring songs. Good music helps prepare the heart for worship. It is like fertilizer for the word. The point is not to get into a style war but to find our favorite styles and become singers during the week: early in the morning, on the way to church, and at church. Good, rich, theological songs are those songs that, when we sing them, we forget about ourselves. Our full focus and attention are directed toward God. It is okay to show emotion towards God when we sing; that is what good theological songs do.

In Christian music recently, there has been a resurgence of some powerful songs that may be helpful to sing before sermons or even on the way to church each week. They are songs that help focus our attention on getting ready to listen to God's word being preached. They help to get hearts ready for the worship of the word. We can talk to our worship leaders and ask them to select songs that help us focus on what is coming, the preaching of God's word.[13] I hope we can find great joy in singing songs that speak toward our desire that his word will change us when it is preached.

One of the best ways I can illustrate the importance of preparing our hearts to come worshipping is through a negative example of myself. The view in my mind's eye is as fresh today as it was then. I was seventeen years old and was driving all alone to camp held that summer between my junior and senior year of high school. I remember thinking to myself as I was getting off the highway, exiting towards Taylor University in Upland, Indiana, "Okay, I need to prepare myself for camp. I guess I should turn off my bad music and turn on something Christian." So I turned off the radio, put in some Christian music, and began to prepare myself. I knew that my youth pastor had been telling me for weeks before this to prepare my heart for camp, but I thought it was not that important. I waited until the last possible moment to prepare my heart.

Many people do the same thing when they come to church. They prepare as they walk through the doors, as they turn into the parking lots, or even as they say quick prayers before the sermon. I missed out on many of the things the Lord wanted to teach me that summer because I was not prepared to worship him. Friends, let us all come worshipping.

Come Praying

When was the last time that before church—maybe on the way, maybe in the morning, maybe before the sermon—or just before the preacher got up to preach, we bowed our hearts and prayed for God to use the words out of the preacher's mouth that week to deal with us in a wonderful, amazing way? When was the last time we asked God before the sermon to enable us to pay attention and to avoid being distracted? When was the last time that we came to the sermon praying that God would open our eyes to behold wonderful things of Him? Once again, the psalmists stand as perfect examples of those who prayed hard that God would open their eyes to understand the wonderful truths of his word. We should pray like the psalmist when he said, "Blessed are You,

---

13. I recommend two songs: "Ancient Words" by Lynn Deshazo and "Speak, O Lord" by Keith Getty and Stuart Townhend.

O LORD; teach me Your statutes" (Ps 119:12) or "Deal bountifully with Your servant, that I may live and keep Your word. Open my eyes, that I may behold wonderful things from Your law" (Ps 119:17–18). How will it change things if we ask God to teach us his statutes? Or if we plead with God to deal bountifully with us that we may live and keep his word. What if we ask God to open our eyes to behold wonderful things from his law? Another example is found in King David. In Psalm 25:4–5, he prayed, "Make me know Your ways, O LORD; teach me Your paths. Lead me in Your truth and teach me, for You are the God of my salvation; for You I wait all the day."

I have a theory about people and their preparation in prayer as they come to the sermon. I think it does not happen as often as it should. I think most people do not come praying for God to do something special in their hearts that week from the sermons preached. My theory is based upon my experience, for I tend not to come praying. I tend to think that listening to the sermon is something I can accomplish on my own. Do you agree? We are independent, proud individuals who think we can do it all ourselves. We seldom have the attitude of the psalmists who prayed those prayers, frankly, because we do not feel as though we need to.

If we chronicle our mental prayers, they may go something like this: "I will teach myself your ways, O Lord. I will make myself know your truth and I will find your paths. I promise to listen and respond to what your servant says." Notice the difference? Probably with all good intentions, we have subtly taken God out of the process and made it something about ourselves. This simply will not do.

A theology of self has warped many good perspectives concerning the need for prayer. Remember, listening to a sermon is ultimately a spiritual event. If it is a spiritual event, then we need God to do something in our lives to understand the spiritual fully. Was it not Jesus himself who said his followers would need the Holy Spirit to lead them into all truth? Remember from chapter 1 that God does his work through his Spirit. Therefore, we need to pray, pray, pray, and pray that God will help. Pray that God will use his Spirit to open our eyes to understand the truth that is being presented. Prayer is crucial. Charles Spurgeon said, "I have always found that the meaning of a text can be better learned by prayer than by any other way. Of course, we must consult lexicons and commentaries to see the literal meaning of the words and their relation to one another. But when we have done all that, we shall still find that our greatest help will come from prayer."[14]

Arthur Bennett's little book called *The Valley of Vision: A Collection of Puritan Prayers and Devotions* is extremely valuable for help in shaping the mind on prayers toward God in this realm. The prayer entitled "The Spirit as Teacher" so adequately expresses what people need to learn about the importance of the Holy Spirit and the need to pray when it comes to understanding the truth:

> O God the Holy Spirit, that which I know not, teach thou me, keep me a humble disciple in the school of Christ, learning daily there what I am in myself, a fallen sinful creature, justly deserving everlasting destruction; O let me never lose sight of my need of a saviour, or forget that apart from him I am nothing, and can do nothing. Open my understanding to know the Holy Scriptures; Reveal to my soul the counsels and works of the blessed Trinity; Instil [sic] into my dark mind the saving knowledge of Jesus ... O lead me into all truth, thou Spirit of wisdom and revelation, that I may know the things that belong unto my peace, and through thee be made anew. Make practical upon my heart the Father's love as thou hast revealed it in the Scriptures ... Thy office is to teach me to draw near to Christ with a pure heart, steadfastly persuaded of his love, in the full assurance of faith. Let me never falter in this way.[15]

That is a good prayer, but maybe we should write our own prayers so that they come from our hearts. Here is an example of one that I often pray before Sunday mornings:

> Heavenly Father, I pray that as I go to church this morning, would you please be gracious to me and allow me to listen, to hear, to understand what is preached. I pray that you would forgive me of my sins, that you would teach me something wonderful this morning. I pray that you would allow me not to be distracted by others and that as I do my part of listening, you would do your part of molding and teaching. I pray that I would leave the service changed. I pray that I would leave as a different person, dealing with what you would have for me to deal with. Thank you for what you are about to do in me this morning.

14. Carter, *2200 Quotations*, 25.
15. Bennett, *Valley of Vision*, 32.

We should pray for ourselves as we go to church, as we go to the sermon table for food. However, there is another issue when it comes to prayer before sermons: We should also pray for our preachers. How many times have we committed to praying throughout the week for our preachers that God will open their eyes as they are studying so that they will be able to apply their sermons to their own lives, that they will know how best to communicate the messages to us, and that they will not get in the way of what God wants to communicate during the sermon. We can go to our preachers and ask them for a list of prayer requests so we can pray for our preachers during the week in regard to their personal lives and their preparation for their sermons. We can ask them to update those prayer requests on a monthly basis and commit to pray for them and their families daily. The Apostle Paul requested, "Brethren, pray for us" (1 Thess 5:25). He also said, "Now I urge you, brethren, by our Lord Jesus Christ and by the love of the Spirit, to strive together with me in your prayers to God for me, that I may be rescued from those who are disobedient in Judea, and that my service for Jerusalem may prove acceptable to the saints; so that I may come to you in joy by the will of God and find refreshing rest in your company. Now the God of peace be with you all. Amen" (Rom 15:30–33). He also said, "Praying at the same time for us as well, that God will open up to us a door for the word, so that we may speak forth the mystery of Christ, for which I have also been imprisoned; that I may make it clear in the way I ought to speak" (Col 4:3–4; see Eph 6:18–19).

If the Apostle Paul needed people to pray for him, I guarantee that pastors, leaders, and preachers need the prayers of their congregants. As we come praying for our own hearts and for our preachers, we will be more ready to receive the word of God as it is preached. Friends, let us all come praying.

Come Expecting

Can it be that one of the reasons sermons have such little impact each week across the pulpits in our world is that people expect so little from them? Can it be that we do not expect God to do anything? A holy expectation was one of the dominant characteristics of the people of the Bible. The prophets of old longed and waited in anticipation for what God might do in their lives. Do we ever think like Micah, the prophet, when he said, "But as for me, I will watch expectantly for the LORD; I will wait for the God of my salvation. My God will hear me" (Mic 7:7). There was an expectation of the coming Messiah.

Then, there is that great account of that faithful man named Simeon in Jerusalem who was looking and waiting for the Messiah to come and restore Israel (Luke 2:25–32). He was told that he would not see death until he had seen the Messiah. Can you imagine, as he got older, how every week in the temple was one of anticipation? He waited for the moment. This was, in some sense, a holy anticipation. On this side of Jesus coming and dying upon the cross and then ascending, people should be anticipating his coming again. That should be the pattern of all true Christians: to wait for Christ to return.

Isaiah prophesied that at Christ's second coming there will be an expectation of his law (Isa 42:4). Paul told Titus that one of the results of Christ coming in the first place was to change people's lives and direct them to "look for the blessed hope and the appearing of the glory of our great God and Savior, Christ Jesus" (Titus 2:13). And while we wait in anticipation, shouldn't there be a sense that we anticipate his word preached and proclaimed?

William Carey, often referred to as the father of modern missions, was well-known for his life motto: "Expect great things from God; Attempt great things for God."[16] What if the church believes and lives a phrase like this when it comes to the preaching of his Word? What if we say, "God, we will attempt great things for you, things like listening intently, avoiding distractions, coming prepared, and so on. And then, God, we expect great things from you, things like life change and heart change; and we expect that you will do something in our lives through the preaching of your Word."

Elizabeth Dodds, in her book chronicling the marriage between Jonathan and Sarah Edwards, wrote about the weekly life of the Puritans in the early 1700s. She adequately described the expectancy that the early Puritans had in regards to the weekly sermon in church:

> Then after three o'clock on Saturday afternoon, the mood of expectancy began to build up to the pivotal day. These people really believed that Sunday would bring encounter with a living and dependable God who had brought them to this new land and watched over their effort to build his holy commonwealth. While a large roast cooked all day, to ensure cold meat for Sunday, a great

---

16. Galli and Olson. *131 Christians*, 245.

> copper tub before the fire held water which was being warmed for baths. Shoes were shined, clothes laid out for the next day, and "modesty pieces" ironed ... Father, abstracted, would be finishing his two sermons for the next day. Then on Saturday night the family sang a psalm together, had prayers, and went upstairs to bed with a sense of anticipating drama, as children now do only on Christmas Eve.[17]

That is somewhat unimaginable. What if we come to the preaching event with expectancy like that of Christmas morning? How will that change our attitudes, our attendance, our tardiness, and our expectations?

I still remember being a child at Christmas time and not being able to sleep the night before. I remember lying in bed wondering if the night would ever end. I remember thinking about what was going to happen, dreaming about what I might get for Christmas, and pondering what I was going to do with what I got.

I have a confession: I still get that same sort of anticipation, only it is not for Christmas morning (being a parent, I would enjoy sleeping in that morning). No, my anticipation is for golf. If I know that I am playing a nice golf course early one morning, I have a hard time sleeping the night before. I check the weather. I pick out my clothes. I clean off the golf clubs. I lie in bed the night before and think about what clubs I plan on hitting on what holes. I am sure there are things that everyone anticipates as much as I anticipate golf.

Okay, seriously, what if we have those same feelings of anticipation for the sermon? What if we know what the preacher is going to preach on and have looked at it already? What if we just cannot sleep because we are so excited that tomorrow morning we are going to hear God speak to us through the word preached by his messenger? How will that impact how we listen to the sermon that next morning?

I went to a Christian school from kindergarten through my junior year in high school. For many reasons, I switched schools my senior year. When I did, it quickly became apparent to me that there was one major difference in how I viewed church and the word of God being preached. After not being around Christian things all day, I came to church on Sundays and for midweek services because I needed to do so to get through the week, not simply because I was supposed to come. These were not just other days for me; they were special. I began to grow

---

17. Dodds, *Marriage to a Difficult Man*, 54–55.

in anticipation of what God wanted to do in my heart every week and was ready for it. Christian, this is how we should come to the sermon, with the expectation that in that sermon God is going to do something special in our lives. It is not just another sermon. Friends, let us all come expecting.

Come Forgiving

If there is one thing that we need to learn in our churches across America, it is what it means really to forgive others. It is amazing that almost every married couple that comes into my office for counseling will at some point show evidence that one of them struggles with forgiving the other person. For some reason, people really struggle with forgiveness. Maybe that is why songs in the Christian music industry that focus on the forgiveness of Christ are so popular. People can appreciate his forgiveness, for they know how hard it is for them to forgive others. Let me make a plea: Please forgive others. More specifically, please forgive your pastors.

A recent study of listeners to sermons indicated that listeners tend to hold things against their preachers. In relaying their findings, the authors stated,

> If the preacher does not walk the walk (live in ways that are consistent with the gospel), many in the congregation will not pay full attention to the talk (sermon). As one interviewee puts it, "If they don't walk the walk, then nobody's going to listen to them when they talk the talk. Walking the walk is really critical" . . . We note that some listeners say that not "walking the walk" undermines the willingness to pay attention to the sermon, and we comment on the danger that can linger in congregations when trust between preacher and people is lost.[18]

Can I just ask a very blunt question? Do we hold grudges against our preachers? Do we have something against them? George Whitefield gives this warning:

> Take heed therefore, my brethren, and beware of entertaining any dislike against those whom the Holy Ghost has made overseers over you. Consider that the clergy are men of like passions with yourselves; and though we should even hear a person teaching others to do, what he has not learned himself; yet, that is no suf-

18. Mulligan and Allen, *Make the Word*, 15.

ficient reason for rejecting his doctrine: for ministers speak not in their own, but Christ's name. And we know who commanded the people to do whatsoever the Scribes and Pharisees should say unto them, though they said but did not.[19]

Certainly a word can be spoken to preachers here to make certain that their lives and messages are in line; but because this book is not addressed to preachers but to listeners, let me exhort all of us to never hold things against our preachers. Listen to the words, not to the men; and as they align with the Holy Scriptures, listen to them and obey them. I do not know what they have done, but do not hold things against them. Effective listeners to sermons cannot hold something against the persons who are the mouthpieces of God.

We may have hurt feelings against our preachers. Maybe they never called us when we were going through the loss of loved ones. Maybe they were a little too harsh to us when we were dealing with those sin issues. Maybe they pushed us too hard into ministry and made us feel as if we do not do enough. The list can keep going, but we must realize that ministers, pastors, and preachers are just human, which means they sin. If anyone, outside of our spouses, needs our forgiveness the most, it is probably our pastors, our preachers. So let's forgive them.

How do I know this? Because I live in the world of preacher and listener. As I have already noted in the introduction, the majority of my weeks are spent in the pew just like everyone else. But there are many times over the course of the year that I do step into the pulpit and preach. I teach every week in many settings, so I live both as a preacher and a listener. I can tell you that I need the forgiveness of the people who listen to me, and I assume that most preachers do as well. I was just listening to a sermon this past week in which a famous preacher in America was asking his church for forgiveness for not emphasizing the grace of God in their lives and preaching too harshly towards them. Speaking as a preacher, we need you to forgive us. Speaking as a listener, I hope I never hold anything against my preacher that will cause me not to listen to what he is saying from God's word.

There is one additional word about preachers and forgiveness. Most of the preachers and teachers I know are quick to seek forgiveness if they have any idea that they have offended anyone. But honestly, they probably have no idea. Please talk to them. Please never hold something

---

19. Whitefield, "Sermon 28," lines 89–92.

against them that they have no idea they have done. Reveal their offenses and give them the opportunity to make things right. Peter told his people to keep fervent in their "love for one another, because love covers a multitude of sins (1 Pet 4:8). Congregants need to love because love will cover; it will move them to forgive sins.

The church is in trouble if it does not have the love that covers sins. Why? Because it is filled with sinners. Yes, redeemed sinners but still sinners. Everyone sins. If people in the church hold onto the sins that other people commit and keep bringing them back to them, holding them over their heads, they can really mess up the church. This means we cannot hold grudges; we do not hold on to the sin. It means that true love forgives and forgives and forgives. It means that if we hold something against our preachers, we will *not* listen with open, honest, expectant hearts.

But there is more than just forgiving our preachers. Are there others in our churches, at our work, in our families right now that we have not forgiven? Are there others who have something against us, and we have not gone to them to make things right? Do not think that this will not hinder our listening and learning from the sermon. It will!

The Bible makes it very clear that relationships with other people in bad standing will affect worship. Jesus gave a scenario that everyone can relate to: "If you are presenting your offering at the altar, and there remember that your brother has something against you, leave your offering there before the altar and go; first be reconciled to your brother, and then come and present your offering" (Matt 5:23–24). This does not mean that we should not come to church or offer our sacrifices (of worship) because we cannot deal with our brothers. It means that we should deal with those relationships. We need to come to sermons forgiving. We need to come and listen to our preachers with clear consciences. Individuals will never be more like God than when they forgive like Christ. Recently I had a hard situation of forgiveness in my life with a friend of mine. I simply came to the conclusion that the best way I could be godly in my relationship with him was to forgive him the way Christ had forgiven me.

Let me finish this section with an admonition to think of forgiveness in some really special terms. The best way to overcome our struggles with forgiveness is to think of the things that have been done in offense to us. Sure, add them up. Take all the offenses other persons have heaped upon us and then take those hurt feelings and multiply them by an infinite amount. That is what we have done to God just today because of our sins. Yet Christ stands to offer complete, whole, absolute forgiveness for all of those sins.

Forgiveness is truly amazing! Some of us should probably stop reading this book to go forgive people we have been holding grudges against. Come back and read later, but forgive them today! Be like Jesus! If we are believers reading this, then we have to realize that Christ still stands by us when we sin. He is not holding it over our heads to bring it back up to us when we mess up again. If you are an unbeliever, I want you to know that no matter what you have done, no matter what has happened to you, Jesus Christ can forgive you of all your sins. You will never out-sin the grace of God in Christ Jesus.

It is about time that, as Christians, we mark ourselves as being forgiving people. Read the texts of Scripture on forgiveness. Read books that are written on forgiveness. Coming to the table of God's word with bitterness or hatred or anger in our hearts towards someone else will keep us from learning what God wants us to learn. Friends, let us all come forgiving.

A few years ago, our senior pastor was invited to speak at a youth camp that many of the young people from our church were attending. The week before the camp, I asked our pastor what he planned to teach. He said that he was taking some of the things that he had preached in church a few months ago. The camp seemed to go well, and many of those students came home lit on fire by God and from what God had taught them through the preaching of his word that week at camp.

We offered a special share time one Sunday night after they returned for the students to talk about what they had learned. Guess what they said? Almost all of them talked about how awesome it was that their pastor had changed the messages he had preached in church and made them more for youth. Honestly, I almost started to laugh right there in my seat in church. Why? I looked at him and just knew it, for I have done the same thing. He preached the same sermons, changing very little: same messages, same audience, same preacher, different results. Why? Because they were more prepared to hear from God than on those average Sunday mornings. The distractions of everyday life were gone. God spoke at that camp in the exact same way that he had spoken at church the previous Sundays, but this time the students were listening.

I really despise those church signs with little clever sayings, so I surprise myself that I am even quoting one. But the other day, I drove by one that said, "If you want to hear God speaking, turn down the volume on the world." That is what these students did at camp. They turned down the volume of the world and heard God speaking through the preaching of his word in a new and fresh way. If only we may live every week as if it is camp, if only our ears are ready to listen, if only the distractions of everyday life are gone, we will be amazed at how God will speak to us through the preaching of his word!

What happens after we prepare ourselves to receive the preaching of God's word? That is the subject of the next chapter.

3

Examine the Preaching of God's Word

IN GREEK MYTHOLOGY, THERE is a legendary story of the city of Troy and the Trojan horse. According to Greek mythology, the Trojan War was fought as a result of the kidnapping of Helen of Sparta by the people of Troy. The Greek armies came up against the city of Troy and laid siege to it. For over ten years, the Greeks tried and tried to break into the city with no success. Finally, the Greek army under the direction of Odysseus came up with a brilliant plan of attack. They built a large wooden horse that was hollow inside and filled it with Greek soldiers. The remaining soldiers burned their camps, making it look as if they were leaving, and left the large wooden horse at the gate of the city as a special gift. It was common in those days for the losing general to give the victorious general a horse as a victory prize. The Greeks then set sail in their boats, only going a short distance away, however.

What happened lives in infamy. The people of Troy looked at the horse as a peace gift and gladly accepted it into their city. Later that night, the people had a celebration, for they had won the war. It was a party filled with drinking and dancing. After the people had gone to sleep that night, those inside the horse slipped out and opened the gates so that the army, which had returned after dark, could get inside. Once the gate was open and the Greek armies were inside, it was easy to take down the drunken armies of Troy. The term *Trojan horse* has become known as a term to describe a gift given with ulterior motives or something that looks like one thing but really is another.

This story often stands as a negative example of what it means to be discerning. Many people are like those in the city of Troy: Thinking everything is perfect, they let their guards down and soon are quick, easy targets for error. So it is in the church. Many of us lack discernment, failing to realize that one of our callings in listening to the preaching of God's word is to examine the preaching we listen to each week. All Christians are called to examine all things that claim to be truth. Therefore, after we come prepared to the sermon and give the word of God an audience, the next logical step in listening to preaching is to use discernment to examine that preaching to ensure that we are not being taken captive by any Trojan horses.

After the Apostle Paul left the city of Thessalonica, he went to the city of Berea (Acts 17:10). Once there, Paul went straight into the synagogue of the Jews and started preaching Jesus. Luke recorded that as Paul preached to these people, they "were more noble-minded than those in Thessalonica, for they received the word with great eagerness, examining the Scriptures daily to see whether these things were so" (Acts 17:11). They examined the Scriptures daily to see whether the things that were told to them were true or not. They regarded the Scriptures as the authoritative test of truth. Man's words were measured by God's words.

Their noble-mindedness or, as some translations have it, open-mindedness in comparison with the Thessalonians was evident for two reasons. First, they received the word with great eagerness. They were excited to hear the message Paul was preaching, yet their eagerness did not mean they were gullible. James Montgomery Boice said, "When verse 11 says that they received the message with great eagerness, it does not mean that they were naïve and simply believed everything they heard. It means that unlike those in some of the other cities these people were open to the gospel and had not prejudged it. In other cities the people tended to regard the gospel as something to be rejected out-of-hand, just because it was new. The Bereans instead said: This sounds good. We'd like to hear more about it. Let's listen."[1]

The second reason they were commended for being open-minded was that they searched the Scriptures daily to see if what Paul was saying was accurate. They were eager to hear truth. They wanted to know that what Paul was saying was not some new invention but was actually confirmed in the Scriptures. They "examined" the Scriptures. The word used is the Greek term *anakrino*, a legal term meaning "to investigate" or "to make a judgment call" on something. It means to put something through a rigorous pursuit of the truth. It is the same term used in Pilate's examination of Jesus in regard to the accusations made against

---

1. Boice, *Acts*, 292.

him (Luke 23:13-15). The Bereans listened with eagerness to the message of the Apostle Paul and then tested, examined, or investigated what he said with the text of the Scriptures (for them, the Old Testament) on a daily basis.

Remember that Paul in his journeys went into the synagogues and preached the gospel of Jesus Christ on the Sabbaths. According to the Scriptures, he also met with people daily, both formally in the synagogue and informally in homes and market places, talking about Jesus. As often as Paul spent time with them, both formally and informally, the Berean people searched or examined what he said, comparing it to the Scriptures to ensure it was biblically accurate. From that time, the term *Bereans* has been used to denote those who cherish the biblical doctrine of discernment, those who study the Bible with eagerness to examine what is true and what is false.

It should be noted that their listening was intrinsically linked to their examination. In fact, the two actions are so closely linked that it is impossible to examine truth properly if one does not listen properly. Taken together, they form what I call "discernment listening," listening that happens with an ear for the truth.

It may be helpful at this point to give a working definition of discernment. What does it mean to examine the preaching heard from the pulpit or in the living room? There are many good yet slightly different definitions. John MacArthur said that "discernment is the ability to understand, interpret, and apply truth skillfully.[2] In his book, *The Discipline of Spiritual Discernment*, Tim Challies defined discernment as "the skill of understanding and applying God's Word with the purpose of separating truth from error and right from wrong.[3] Jay Adams also offered a helpful definition when he said that "discernment is skill in reaching understanding and knowledge by the use of a process of separation . . . it is the divinely given ability to distinguish God's thoughts and ways from all others."[4] Looking at what the Bereans did, a good working definition is simply this: *Discernment is the ability to examine and distinguish truth from error.* This definition will be dissected throughout this chapter and referred to several times.

---

2. MacArthur, *Reckless Faith*, xv.
3. Challies, *Discipline of Spiritual Discernment*, 61.
4. Adams, *Call for Discernment*, 46–49.

How are we to listen with a discerning ear? How are we to be like the Bereans in listening to the preaching of God's word? The rest of this chapter will detail principles for discernment listening.

LISTEN ALERTLY

If we want to become effective, discerning listeners, we must be aware that truth and error are both real and exist not only in the world but also in the church. If discernment is the ability to examine and distinguish truth from error, intrinsically there is an assumption that truth and error exist and that there is a distinction between them. It seems the only absolute truth today is that there is no absolute truth. Postmodern society loves truth, just not truth that says that others are wrong. Even within the church, this has crept in subtly, like the Trojan horse, and has made people think that it is wrong to say that other people do not have truth. Jay Adams said,

> God's people were expected to be concerned every day about all they did—even in the little things. They were to go through life distinguishing God's way from what is not God's way. Yet today such biblical thinking has been replaced by a mentality that permits no sharp contrasts. All is gray: There is no black or white, good or bad, right or wrong . . . There is no right and wrong or true and false, but only shades of right and wrong or true and false spread along a continuum. The poles of this continuum are extended so far out toward the wings that for all practical purposes they are unattainable and therefore worthless. Nothing, then, is wholly right or wrong.[5]

Adams wrote that over twenty years ago, and today it applies even more.

But those concepts of truth and error cannot be further from the biblical concepts. According to the Bible, there are always two ways, two paths, or two options: God's truth and not God's truth! This is why listeners to preaching need to listen alertly, for truth assumes error exists.

There are two main terms used in the Bible for discernment. In the Old Testament, it is the Hebrew word *bin*; in the New Testament, it is the Greek term *diakrino*. In distinguishing this terminology, Adams noted,

---

5. Ibid., 20–21, 30.

> The Hebrew term *bin*, which is used 247 times in the Old Testament, has been translated in various ways—"understand, discern, distinguish." It is related to the noun *bayin*, which means "interval" or "space between," and the preposition *ben*, "between." In essence it means to separate things from one another at their points of difference in order to distinguish them.[6]

The Greek term *diakrino* also has the meaning of separation but is used in the sense of judging or making distinctions. These terms help in defining discernment, the ability to examine and distinguish truth from error. It is separating. It is showing the difference. It means that there are two opposing views and a line should be drawn between them.

The Scriptures show over and over again that Christians should be willing to draw lines in the sand when it comes to truth. In Matthew 7:13–27, Jesus made the concept of separation abundantly clear. In verses 13–14, Jesus said there are only two gates, two ways, two destinations, and two groups of people. In verses 15–23, Jesus said there are only two trees and two types of fruit. In verses 24–27, Jesus said there are only two foundations, two men, and two results. Jesus' point is that there is God's way or not God's way. There are only two teams playing in this game.

Jesus is not the only one to say that error and truth coexist. Throughout the New Testament, this concept is explicitly stated. There is always a warning that where there is truth, there will be error. When Paul said goodbye to the elders in Ephesus, he told them that after he left there would be savage wolves that would come in and speak false things to rip the disciples away from them (Acts 20:28–30). It is important to notice that Paul said the false teachers would arise from within their own flock.

Do typical church attendees ever think that their churches, their pastors, their teachers can ever teach something that is untrue? Probably most do not, yet they should consider this. Our preachers are only human. That is why we need to make certain we listen alertly. However, even to suggest that our churches could be in error or that our preachers could be teaching untruth often comes with drastic consequences. John MacArthur, who for so long has stood for the truth, spoke of the normal response to those who separate truth from error: "Even to suggest that a sorting between lies and truth is necessary is viewed by many as perilously intolerant. There is a notion abroad that any dispute over doctrine

---

6. Ibid., 46.

Examine the Preaching of God's Word 71

is inherently evil. Concern for orthodoxy is regarded as incompatible with Christian unity. Doctrine itself is labeled divisive and those who make doctrine an issue are branded uncharitable. No one is permitted to criticize anyone else's beliefs, no matter how unbiblical those beliefs seem to be."[7] Paul wrote that the times for false teachers will go from bad to worse (2 Tim 3:13), which means that Christians should not be shocked that their culture is becoming less and less tolerant of the truth of God.

There is one part of the story of Paul's relationship to Thessalonica that has been left out up to this point. After Paul spent time in Berea, he left. A few months later, he wrote the book of First Thessalonians. In this letter, he commended them in the church for their reception of the word of God (1 Thess 2:13), but he also told them that they needed to be more like the Bereans in the way they discerned the truth: "Do not quench the Spirit; do not despise prophetic utterances. But examine everything carefully; hold fast to that which is good; abstain from every form of evil" (1 Thess 5:19–22).

Prophecies refer to the preaching of divine counsels under the immediate inspiration of the Spirit. The prophets were the human channels through which the Spirit made known his will and purposes for his people. The basic function of the prophets was to speak forth the counsel of God. The understanding of this issue has continued to be debated in many denominations (whether the gift of prophecy still occurs today). However, both sides agree that one aspect of a prophetic ministry in the church is the proclamation of God's message for his people as gathered from the inspired Scriptures under the illumination of the Spirit, not the disclosure of new revelation directly from the Spirit. It is preaching.

Paul, by way of contrast, told them not to despise these utterances but to be careful in their listening. They needed to be Bereans. He told them to examine everything. He said that they were not to mindlessly listen to everything they heard, assuming that because it is coming out of the mouth of someone they assume is godly that the teaching is godly. Rather, they were to take what was said and compare it, investigate it according to the Scriptures. It was to be evaluated. Paul was probably still in awe that there was a group of people who examined his teaching and thought that that would be a good exercise for all listeners to engage in doing. Adams commented, "Surely, if Luke commends those Jews who

---

7. MacArthur, *Reckless Faith*, 20.

eagerly sought to find God's truth by using the Bible as their Standard for judging whether the teaching of Paul, an inspired apostle, was true, how much more important is it to evaluate what TV evangelists, writers of books (including this one), and other uninspired persons teach today!"[8]

The nitty gritty of examining will be discussed in more detail later. For now notice the outcome that Paul desired after the Thessalonians examined everything carefully. They were to hold fast to that which was good and abstain from that which was evil. Paul was telling them that as they listened to teaching, prophetic utterances, and preaching that there would be some that were true and some that were false.

That continues to be true. The only way we will know what is good from what is evil is by examining it according to the Scriptures. Once that is done, we are to hold onto that which is good and get rid of that which is false. And so we listen alertly, knowing that whenever individuals open their mouths and declare truth, there is the chance that it is false.

At this point, many people may feel saddened or overburdened. We may be questioning ourselves: "Who am I? How can I judge or separate or distinguish what anyone says, let alone my pastor. He is the professional. He went to seminary. I am just an ordinary person." There is the temptation that we may throw our arms up in the air and wonder if truth can ever be known at all. If that is so, God has us right where he wants us. Friends, let us listen alertly.

LISTEN PRAYERFULLY

If we want to be faithful, discerning listeners, we will ask the Lord for help. But how many people actually pray for it? How many people ever pray before they listen to teaching or before their preachers get up to preach that they do not become susceptible to something that is false? In the previous chapter, I recommended that before coming to the sermon, we should pray that God will do something amazing in our hearts as the word of God is opened. Now, specifically, we should pray for help in discernment and the ability to separate truth from error. We need help from our Lord. There are two passages of Scripture that help with this, one by way of illustration and one by way of command.

---

8. Adams, *Call for Discernment*, 71.

The illustration is of King Solomon. His story began when the Creator God of the universe, who is much greater than any fictional genie in any story, appeared to Solomon and said, "Ask what you wish me to give you" (1 Kgs 3:5). In response, Solomon reviewed and reiterated to God what had happened in the past (vv. 6–8). He talked about his father, David, to whom God was more than generous. In fact, it was God's generosity to David that allowed Solomon even to sit upon that throne as the King of Israel. He said that he was a little child, not meaning that he was young in age but that compared to the task that he was to accomplish in judging the nation of Israel, he felt like a little child. Many scholars believe that Solomon was just over twenty years old at this time, which is certainly young to be the king. According to John Davis and John Whitcomb, "The expression 'I am but a little child' does not mean that Solomon was a young boy when he took the throne . . . for 'little child' is merely an assertion of humility and a recognition that from the standpoint of experience, he was like a child."[9] It was not only his inexperience or his youthfulness that moved him to seek and ask for wisdom and discernment, but it was his youthfulness compared to the vast number of people that he was now in charge of. To be young, inexperienced, and in charge of many people was a dangerous combination.

What did he ask for? Solomon prayed, "Give your servant an understanding heart to judge Your people to discern between good and evil. For who is able to judge this great people of Yours" (v. 9). He prayed for an "understanding (or listening, hearing) heart." Specifically, that meant a heart that would know the heart of God's law and know how to apply that law to the events that would take place under his leadership. Notice that the outcome of this hearing heart was that he would have discernment to distinguish between that which was false and that which was true. Obviously, Solomon must have been wise to some extent already to know that he was incapable and needed help. Most twenty-year olds would not ask for this thing. As Tim Challies noted, "Solomon was given wisdom, to be sure, but he was also given a hearing heart. He was given discernment such as no mere human has possessed before or since. We might even say that Solomon requested discernment, but because of the connectedness of wisdom and discernment, God gave him both what

---

9. Davis and Whitcomb, *Israel,* 334.

he requested and its important prerequisite. Solomon became both wise and discerning.[10]

It is easy to see the humility and emotion that flowed out of the heart of Solomon. He was looking at his task and thinking it was impossible. He must have thought, "My father was amazing. He did it so well. What am I going to do?" Then God appeared and said to ask anything. That was easy enough for Solomon: "Give me the heart that I need to be able to discern that which is right and that which is wrong." This is why it is important in discernment listening to listen prayerfully. After we understand that there is truth and error mixed together in the world and in the church, we can be easily overwhelmed like Solomon. We need to become like Solomon and cry out, "Dear God, give your servant an understanding heart so that I might be able to discern between that which is right or wrong, that which is true or false. God, I need your help!" God wants his people to be completely dependent upon him.

What was the outcome for Solomon? The one thing that he is known for more than anything else is that, other than Jesus, he was the wisest man to ever live. God's response to Solomon was amazing:

> It was pleasing in the sight of the Lord that Solomon had asked this thing. God said to him, "Because you have asked this thing and have not asked for yourself long life, nor have asked riches for yourself, nor have you asked for the life of your enemies, but have asked for yourself discernment to understand justice, behold, I have done according to your words. Behold, I have given you a wise and discerning heart, so that there has been no one like you before you, nor shall one like you arise after you. I have also given you what you have not asked, both riches and honor, so that there will not be any among the kings like you all your days." (1 Kgs 3:10–13)

God gave him the discernment he asked for and much more. Later in his life, Solomon wrote to his son concerning wisdom and discernment: "My son, if you will receive my words and treasure my commandments within you, make your ear attentive to wisdom, incline your heart to understanding; for if you cry for discernment, lift your voice for understanding; if you seek her as silver and search for her as for hidden treasures; then you will discern the fear of the LORD and discover the knowledge of God. For the LORD gives wisdom; from His mouth come knowledge

---

10. Challies, *Discipline of Spiritual Discernment*, 21.

and understanding." (Prov 2:1-6). Solomon knew that it is the Lord who gives discernment and knowledge. He knew that the Lord wants to give them to those who seek and ask for them. He knew it because he lived it; it happened to him. As Challies said, Solomon's story teaches us "God values discernment and honors those who seek after it."[11]

Will we ever pray for the wisdom to discern preaching? Will we listen to sermons with prayerful hearts, asking God to give us the discernment that we need? Christians should never listen to any sermon, even by those people they trust, without praying that God will give them discernment for the truth in the material that they are about to hear. It does not matter if the preacher is the greatest radio preacher or our own pastors, we should pray that God will give us wisdom and discernment.

Some may make the objection that this (Solomon) was a special case in a special time and that God does not look to special requests for discernment like that anymore. Someone may well object that the story of someone who asks does not necessitate that we should always ask. That may be true, but there is a second passage in which we are commanded to seek after wisdom and discernment. James writes, "But if any of you lacks wisdom, let him ask of God, who gives to all generously and without reproach, and it will be given to him. But he must ask in faith without any doubting, for the one who doubts is like the surf of the sea, driven and tossed by the wind. For that man ought not to expect that he will receive anything from the Lord, being a double-minded man, unstable in all his ways" (James 1:5–8).

The context deals with the trials that people go through (vv. 2–4), so most people believe that the wisdom asked for is the wisdom to understand the reasons for the trials. Although true, the implication of asking for help in discernment or wisdom amidst trials only is short selling the command to pray for wisdom and discernment. It may specifically mean during trials, but the command also has implications to pray for wisdom and discernment during other times as well. James began by addressing anyone who has a need ("if any of you lacks wisdom"). Therefore, if listeners of sermons have need of wisdom, this command applies to them. Well-known commentator D. Edmond Hiebert remarked,

> As a Jew, James viewed wisdom as related to the practice of righteousness in daily life. It is the moral discernment that enables the believer to meet life and its trials with decisions and actions

11. Ibid., 21.

> consistent with God's will . . . James has just set forth a piece of such wisdom in verses 2–4 in relation to the trials of life, but this wisdom has a wider application and relates to all areas of conduct where such discernment is needed. The fear of the Lord is the beginning of such wisdom (Prov 9:10), for the wise man recognizes that he is morally accountable to God for all his decisions and actions in life. This consciousness prompts him to turn to the eternal fountain of wisdom in all circumstances of life.[12]

When we need discernment, we should run to the one who gives generously. But there is a condition in how we ask, for we need to ask with faith and with confidence that he will reward the asking. The analogy in the middle of the passage exemplifies the men and women who ask but do not really mean it. Those persons who doubt God will actually give them the discernment they need are like the sea amidst an angry storm, tossed here and there by the wind. They are considered unstable and double-minded. But those who will receive the wisdom are the ones who ask in faith, without doubting. And God promises that he will give it to those who ask in this way. What James did not say is when it will be given, but we can trust that God will give wisdom and discernment in his perfect time.

Maybe the question should be turned around. If we need discernment about how to behave or what to believe and do not ask, do we trust in God or in ourselves? Hiebert advised, "Any failure to ask implies that the believer is blind to his need, but he who has a constant longing for wisdom will persistently pray for it."[13]

God wants us to ask for discernment in areas of our lives. He even wants us to listen to sermons and read books with prayerful hearts, asking him for help to know what is true and what is false. John MacArthur said, "Although God has wisdom in abundance and is infinitely more willing to impart his wisdom than we are to ask for it, He nevertheless expects us to ask Him for it. It is not something that the Lord will impress on an unwilling heart and mind."[14] After Solomon asked, his request was said to be pleasing in the sight of the Lord (1 Kgs 3:10). It will also be pleasing in the sight of the Lord if we listen to sermons praying for wisdom. Friends, let us listen prayerfully.

12. Hiebert, *James*, 69.
13. Ibid., 69–70.
14. MacArthur, *James*, 36.

LISTEN SPIRITUALLY

Examining the preaching of God's word at its core is a spiritual exercise. Although there may be some physical components, ultimately we are trying to discern spiritual truth from spiritual error. This is not the same as discerning some chemical equation or determining whether two plus two actually does equal four. It is looking at things claimed to be of God to know for certain whether they truly are from him. Because it is spiritual, there is a close connection between the person who is a believer and the Holy Spirit, who is given as the ignition of the heart to understand that which is true and that which is false. In chapter 1, under The Theology of Preaching and Preachers, we noted that God ultimately does his work through his Spirit. Jesus promised his followers that when he left, he would not leave them alone but would send the Holy Spirit to be not only with them but in them: "I will ask the Father, and He will give you another Helper, that He may be with you forever; that is the Spirit of truth, whom the world cannot receive, because it does not see Him or know Him, but you know Him because He abides with you and will be in you" (John 14:16–17; see John 15:26–27).

There are several implications concerning the relationship between the Holy Spirit and the pursuit of truth. *First, the Holy Spirit is the Spirit of Truth.* Truth is one of the designations that Jesus gives to the Holy Spirit. He is also called the Comforter and Helper, but the designation that is given to this helper or comforter is that he is "of truth." John Calvin said that by the designation of "Spirit of truth . . . people who do not have this witness get carried away all over the place and have no firm resting-place; but wherever the Spirit speaks, he sets people's minds free from all doubt and fear of being deceived."[15] It is because of his quality of truth that his role is then to help impart that truth of God into the disciples (and all other Christians).

Jesus explained more in just a few short verses: "These things I have spoken to you while abiding with you. But the Helper, the Holy Spirit, whom the Father will send in My name, He will teach you all things, and bring to your remembrance all that I said to you" (John 14:25–26). Boice remarked that the "Holy Spirit teaches us as well, and the Holy Spirit is the One who brings these things to our remembrance."[16] His role as the

---

15. Calvin, *John*, 368.
16. Boice, *Gospel of John*, 1148.

Spirit of Truth is to come and teach us, the followers of Jesus, about the truth of God. He will lead us into all truth.

Second, without the Spirit, truth cannot be discerned or known. It is impossible to be a discerning person without the Spirit of Truth. This is the argument that Paul made in 1 Corinthians 2:11–14, that the natural man (unbeliever) cannot accept the things of the Spirit of God. It is foolishness to him. Now this does not mean that the unbeliever can never find truth. It does not mean that the unbeliever cannot ever know that something spiritual is true and something is false. For instance, there are many who acknowledge that Jesus Christ is the only way for salvation, but they simply are not willing to give their lives over to him. When Paul wrote this, he was not saying that it is never possible for any unbeliever to understand some biblical truth. What he was saying is that although natural unbelievers may excel past believers in many things in life, they will never excel in the truth of God. They may be greater in their understanding of sociology, in the truth of mathematics, in the truths of philosophy, or in the truths of education; but without the Spirit of Truth that encompasses the truth of the spiritual things of God, unbelievers will never outshine believers in their ability to discern truth from error.

Speaking of the natural man, Simon Kistemaker vividly remarked,

> With respect to spiritual matters, he is like a man who flips the switch during an electrical power failure and receives no light. Worse, he has no idea what caused the failure and is unable to predict the duration of the blackout. He is powerless to alter the situation but must wait until the electrical supply is restored. Similarly, unless the Spirit's power enters his life and enlightens him spiritually, he remains in spiritual darkness. The Holy Spirit enables man to see clearly the path that leads to life and to evaluate accurately the circumstances in which he finds himself.[17]

It bears repeating: If we want to be good listeners to sermons, we must start with salvation. We can listen alertly, knowing that there is something called truth and something called error out there in this world. We can listen prayerfully, crying out to God that he will give us discerning hearts. But unless we listen spiritually by seeking after salvation first, those first two and all to follow will be useless.

Practically, then, what role does the Holy Spirit have in preaching events, in listening to sermons? John Calvin put these two things to-

---

17. Kistemaker, *1 Corinthians*, 92.

gether when he said, "Outward preaching will be vain and useless if it is not accompanied by the Spirit's teaching. God therefore has two ways of teaching: first, he sounds in our ears by human speech; and second, he addresses us inwardly by his Spirit. He does this either simultaneously or at different times, as he thinks fit."[18]

Should we then just sit back and let the Spirit do it? Or, in some way, does the Spirit of God, who reveals and illumines the truth, work in cooperation with us whom he indwells? I argue against the notion of "let go and let God," for in some way the child of God must have some responsibility in the discernment of truth. The answer lies here: If the Spirit of Truth is the one that helps us understand and discern truth from error, then we need to understand how we should be in relation to the Holy Spirit.

In 1 Thessalonians 5:19, we are instructed to "not quench the Spirit." In Ephesians 4:30, we are told to "not grieve the Holy Spirit of God." We are not to stand in opposition to what the Spirit wants us to do. This has to do with the holiness of everyday life. The Holy Spirit is often seen as a visible picture of fire throughout the Bible; thus, "quench" means to put the fire out. When we do that, when we ignore the promptings of the Holy Spirit in our lives in regards to our personal holiness, we are quenching and thereby grieving the Holy Spirit. The Spirit is grieved anytime we violate the will of God in our lives.

Then how are we to act? Instead of quenching or grieving, we are to be filled with the Spirit. The Apostle Paul gave this analogy, which helps in understanding what it means to be filled with the Spirit: "Do not get drunk with wine, for that is dissipation, but be filled with the Spirit" (Eph 5:18). The filling of the Spirit does not mean that we get more of the Spirit as in the sense of filling a glass with water. The metaphor of wine indicates what Paul means here. In the same way wine takes over individuals when they are drunk and makes them do things that are not normal to them, the Holy Spirit should take over or control believers so that what is normal for them (sin) will not be evident. We do not get more of the Spirit; the Spirit simply gets more of us.

To be filled with the Spirit is to be under his control. We should be asking, "Who controls me? Am I letting the Spirit of God dictate and control my heart and actions or do I desire to still be in control?" In having the Spirit of God control our lives, we will then walk by him. The

18. Calvin, *John*, 349.

things of God and his Spirit will dictate the paths of our lives: "But I say, walk by the Spirit, and you will not carry out the desire of the flesh" (Gal 5:16). This will then result in the fruit of the Spirit being evident in our lives (Gal 5:22–23).

What is the point of this? How is this linked to discernment in listening to preaching in our lives? There seems to be a direct link between the Spirit of God having control of our lives and our ability to discern truth from error. We will never effectively listen spiritually if we are walking lives that are contrary to the Holy Spirit, which will make the ability to cut accurately through and separate that which is true and false very difficult, probably impossible. Friends, let us listen spiritually.

LISTEN ENERGETICALLY

Discernment is not easy and takes some hard work. If we really desire to develop the ability to examine and distinguish truth from error, it is going to take some holy sweat. The author of Hebrews spoke about the hard work that it takes to be a discerning person. "Concerning him we have much to say, and it is hard to explain, since you have become dull of hearing. For though by this time you ought to be teachers, you have need again for someone to teach you the elementary principles of the oracles of God, and you have come to need milk and not solid food. For everyone who partakes only of milk is not accustomed to the word of righteousness, for he is an infant. But solid food is for the mature, who because of practice have their senses trained to discern good and evil" (Heb 5:11–14).

The reason the author had to once again teach these people the elementary things of the Christian life instead of the more difficult things was because they had become dull of hearing. The word for "dull" is a very unique term in the New Testament. A. T. Robertson said this word originally came from two words: *ne*, which is negative, and *otheo*, which means "to push."[19] So it means literally "no push." The point of "no push" is to signify that they were slow, not pushing their way through something. This term was also used in the Septuagint (Greek translation of Old Testament) in describing the slothful man who refused to tackle hard work.

19. Robertson, *Word Pictures*, 371.

In Hebrews, it is put in its context by the next term, "hearing." Although the word can literally refer to the organ of the ears, the physical ears are not being pushed. The author used the physical ears to represent the people's listening skills. These people were not very good hearers; they did not push to become good listeners. That is why the wording is translated in most versions as "dull of hearing." Their ears have become lazy or sluggish, which is a really good word picture, isn't it?

These people had come to treat the Bible, the truth of God's word, with an "I could care less" attitude. This does not mean that they did not attend church or that they did not bring their Bibles or did not follow along or did not nod their heads or even say amen! It means those things were all they did. It was almost as if the message went in one ear and out the other ear without ever really penetrating and causing learning and understanding to take place. It means that they used no energy in their listening.

The author said that because of their lack of energy in their listening, they had failed to grow spiritually. They ought to have been teachers by that time, but they were not. They had to be taught again the very basics of Christianity. Then the author made the connection between listening that lacks energy and the failure to be discerning persons. They were content with milk; they were infants. They were not "accustomed to the word of righteousness." They were unskilled, untried, or inexperienced in the word of righteousness, which is the message or content that produces correct actions or right living. They did not work hard at understanding. They were content with the status quo in their personal understanding of the message, the truth, the divine truth that leads to godly living. These people had not developed the necessary skills to get past the milk.

Now, compare them with the mature people. What is the difference? They grew and enjoyed solid food. The text says that because of practice they had trained themselves to discern good and evil. This training is very hard work; it is the Greek term *gumnazo* from which the English language gets the word "gymnasium." What usually happens in a gymnasium? Laziness? No. It is usually something that requires energy, discipline, and effort. That is the point. To be persons who listen effectively takes energy. If we desire to be discerning, we must listen energetically. There is no shortcut to being a discerning person. It is going to take the hard work and discipline. It is going to take effort. Some of the principles described later will make apparent what is meant by hard work.

We may ask why discernment is so difficult. Our definition may have been a bit misleading so far. Although it is true that discernment is the ability to examine and distinguish truth from error, if we believe that that is all discernment is, we are misleading ourselves. Charles Spurgeon is famous for saying that "discernment is not a matter of simply telling the difference between right and wrong; rather it is the difference between right and almost right." We often forget that the enemies of the gospel disguise themselves as angels of light (2 Cor 11:13–14). Spurgeon was right: Discernment takes lots of energy because the enemy is not disguising falsehood as something that is the opposite of Christianity but as Christianity.

Can someone run a marathon without ever training? Can someone be a good golfer without every playing? Can someone be an Olympic athlete without ever going to the gym and working at the chosen sport? Can someone ever be a good salesperson without working hard to find new clients? Can someone ever lose weight without changing current diets and exercise programs? The answer to all of these questions is obviously no. So it is with discernment. It is going to take hard work and energy to be good, discerning listeners to God's truth being preached. Friends, let us listen energetically.

LISTEN HUMBLY

As we listen to the preaching of God's word, have we ever thought "I have already heard a sermon on this passage? I know what that text means for my life. I know what he is going to say; he simply is repeating himself again. I really disagree with that theological position that I know he is hinting at?" Sound familiar? I want to challenge us that if we ever have these thoughts or similar ones, we are approaching the sermon not with a spirit of humility but with a spirit rooted in pride. If we approach the sermon in pride, we will never be good discerners of truth because we fail to be teachable.

Teachability is one of the keys to being a discerning person. When we understand that truth and error are present, then we cry out to the Lord for help. We rely upon his Spirit to teach us and then begin to work hard at discernment. We are naturally showing we are humble and in need of help. We are showing we are teachable. Solomon cried for his sons to be teachable: "Now therefore, O sons, listen to me, for blessed are they who keep my ways. Heed instruction and be wise, and do not neglect it. Blessed is the man who listens to me, watching daily at my gates, waiting at my doorposts. For he who finds me finds life and obtains favor from the LORD. But he who sins against me injures himself; all those who hate me love death" (Prov 8:32–36).

Like wisdom crying out asking for someone to listen, preachers are calling out, hoping we will listen to what they say. Some of us reading this already think we have everything figured out in the Christian life. We think we have all our theology perfect. We think that we are doing everything right in our walk. Those thoughts will keep us from listening as we should.

Probably the most obvious way this is manifested in our lives is when we listen to sermons thinking they would be perfect for our friends or spouses. We think, "I hope they are listening. They really need this." When we listen to sermons with other people in mind, our focus and attention are not placing us in position to be taught by our preachers. This may not be intentional, but it can be.

For some reason, this problem really is manifested in connection with controversial doctrinal issues. For instance, imagine some individuals struggling with the doctrine of election. Maybe when they hear sermons preached that refer to it, they struggle because it does not sound like what they assumed it is or what they have heard in the past. They have two options. They can sit there and dismiss the topic, saying that their pastors or preachers are wrong; or they can listen with teachable hearts, go home and look up verses, pick up some other literature, and pray for help in understanding the doctrine. Notice the difference? One option (the latter) is a heart that is teachable. The other (the former) is a heart that is obstinate and proud.

Unfortunately, this issue has been manifested in my life with a man at our church who has been struggling through some things that we teach. For some reason, he responds to each sermon negatively because he is only focused on certain issues that he has addressed to me in private. He comes to me almost every week and points out the negative things in the sermons, and I spend time trying to correct his thinking. He is prejudging what our preacher is going to say, and he is not listening to the sermon. Rather, he is picking and choosing the parts to which he listens. Eventually, I pointed out to him that his pride was keeping him from listening effectively. I talked to him about how his pride is keeping him from being teachable. He fails to discern what the preacher is saying because his listening is affected by his lack of teachability.

Many people listen to sermons the way my youngest son, who is seven, drives a golf cart. Occasionally I take him golfing with me and sit him on my lap and let him steer. Every now and then, I have to grab the wheel to keep us from crashing into a bridge or going over a cliff. He will say to me, "Dad, I can do it. Let me do it." What he means is that he does not need my help; he does not need to be taught. So I take these moments to teach him about what he needs. We talk about being teachable. We talk about his need for someone to teach him.

All of us need to be teachable. If we are not, we greatly affect our abilities to discern truth from error. We all have pride problems. Some have even said it is the greatest problem,—not our upbringing, not Satan, but pride. We need to fight our pride by being humble and by growing in humility. C. J. Mahaney said, "God is decisively drawn to humility. The person who is humble is the one who draws God's attention, and in this sense, drawing His attention means also attracting His grace—His unmerited kindness. Think about that: There's something you can do to attract more of God's gracious, undeserved, supernatural strength and assistance!"[20]

Think about it. Can even some of that grace and undeserved supernatural strength and assistance that he talked about be discernment? Be teachable. Be humble. Listen with more and more humility every time we hear a sermon. Friends, let us listen humbly.

LISTEN RELATIONALLY

What are our relationships to our preachers? The more people know their preachers, the better they will be able to listen and discern truth from their sermons. Aristotle has long been credited for his work on the nature of rhetoric or public speaking. He said there are three dynamics that connect a speaker to his audience: "the audience's perception of the person and character of the preacher (ethos), the audience's perception that the speaker has developed the content of the sermon to show that the message of the speech is true (logos), and the audience's response to

---

20. Mahaney, *Humility: True Greatness*, 20.

the feelings and identifications generated in connection with the sermon (pathos)."[21]

The concept of ethos is very important in the listening process. What sort of relationship does the listener have with the preacher or pastor? Will good relationships with their pastors help average persons in the discernment of their sermons? Will the relationships affect the way they hear the preachers' illustrations, the way they take what the pastors say and test it against the Scriptures to see if it is true or not? Earlier in my ministry, I was involved with junior high school students, a real test of any calling to full-time ministry. At our church was a lay helper named Chris. Although he was not a very dynamic teacher, there was something about him. The students loved to listen to him teach. I was unaware of Aristotle at that time, but what I knew from watching him and the students was that when the students had a connection to their leaders, they listened better to them.

According to one survey of listeners, ethos plays a major role in how people listen:

> Seeing that a minister faithfully carries out pastoral practices throughout leadership in the church assures some listeners of the quality of the preaching. An interviewee approves of the minister telling the congregation that the minister is available to talk with members any time. Another links the preacher conducting business in a business-like way with trustworthiness of the sermon. Still another interprets the preacher visiting with members of the congregation in the pews before worship as a sign that the pastor is interested in the congregation. Thinking that the minister is interested in the people prompts this congregant to be more interested in the sermon. A number of interviewees say that the minister's regular visits in their homes raise their attentiveness to the sermon because they have the sense that the preacher has been listening to them.[22]

To be clear, almost all the published material in this area speaks about preachers being concerned about helping the ethos connection with the listeners. That means that preachers should do things to help those connections occur. As a pastor and preacher, it is my responsibility to build relationships with those to whom I minister. But why can't some

---

21. Allen, *Hearing the Sermon*, 6–7.
22. Ibid., 23.

of that responsibility fall upon the listeners? Can we take some of the initiative to spend some time with our preachers to get to know them?

However, we must have real expectations. If we attend a megachurch, we will have very few opportunities to spend time with our preachers. We may have to set up appointments with them several weeks or months in advance, but it will be beneficial for us to do so. If we attend small churches, we should be seeking continual opportunities to get to know our preachers. Whatever the size of our congregations, there are opportunities to build relationships with our preachers. Seek to know them and their families.

The Scriptures are clear that Christians should have respectful relationships with those who are in leadership over them: "Remember those who led you, who spoke the word of God to you; and considering the result of their conduct, imitate their faith" (Heb 13:7). It will be impossible to imitate their faith if we do not know them, if we do not work hard at getting to know them. The author of Hebrews also said, "Obey your leaders and submit to them, for they keep watch over your souls as those who will give an account. Let them do this with joy and not with grief, for this would be unprofitable for you" (Heb 13:17). Paul said, "But we request of you, brethren, that you appreciate those who diligently labor among you, and have charge over you in the Lord and give you instruction, and that you esteem them very highly in love because of their work" (1 Thess 5:12–13).

These passages are often not spoken of from pulpits, for preaching on such passages can appear to be very self-serving. However, these passages and this topic are in the Bible, a calling for all who sit in church to remember, obey, appreciate, and esteem the leaders who are over them. We all need to pray and determine what that means for our families and us. How can we remember, obey, appreciate, and esteem our leaders?

Paul told the people of Corinth to "be imitators of me, just as I also am of Christ" (1 Cor 11:1). How could that happen without some form of relationship between the people and Paul? He said it again to the church at Philippi when he wrote, "Brethren, join in following my example, and observe those who walk according to the pattern you have in us" (Phil 3:17). He also said, "The things you have learned and received and heard and seen in me, practice these things, and the God of peace will be with you" (Phil 4:9).

We can ask questions such as these: Am I doing anything to seek after a relationship with my main preacher? Can I use my home as a tool of ministry to invite him and his family over for dinner? Can I take him and his wife out for dinner simply to get to know them? Is there some sort of activity that I know he enjoys that I can participate in as well to get to know him?

The more we know our preachers, the easier it will be for us to discern what they are teaching and preaching. We will be quicker to forgive them when they seem harsh. We will not be so quick to take things out of context. We will feel greater freedom to ask them questions after sermons about what they said. We will understand their jokes better. Relationship is a key part of this discernment process.

When we begin to build relationships with our preachers, we will find it much easier if we begin by being positive. If we begin a relationship always talking about what is wrong and how negative things are, the relationship will be short lived. Our preachers get that from many other people. If we are positive and encouraging, we will have an open door for more visits and time to build relationships with them and opportunities to ask them questions about their sermons.

However, there is also a word of warning: We should never idolize our spiritual leaders. They are not Jesus. There is only one mediator, and some human preacher is not that mediator (1 Tim 2:2). If we are looking for idols, we should avoid building relationships with our preachers. The closer we get to them, the more faults we will see in them. Even the best of men are still only men.

The greatest way in which we can appreciate and esteem any leader or pastor is by obeying God. It is not about money, cards, lunches, earthly possessions, or anything else that we may do. The greatest way we can esteem our leaders or build relationships with our preachers is to grow in our faith and obedience to God. Then let our preachers know how they have helped in that process. Share specifics with them. Share certain things they have said in their sermons that we have been able to apply and that have helped us grow spiritually. If there are issues that we have in discerning what they have said from the pulpit, pepper the negative questions with some positive statements. Friends, let us all listen relationally.

LISTEN PATIENTLY

Are we patient with our preachers? We should be, for our preachers will fail us. They will sin against us. Paul told the church at Thessalonica to "admonish the unruly, encourage the fainthearted, help the weak, *be patient with everyone*" (1 Thess 5:14, emphasis mine). Everyone includes preachers. What does this mean for us? *First, be patient if our preachers repeat themselves.* Do not get frustrated when our preachers repeat things. Repetition is one of the keys to learning. If the preacher repeats often, it may be that there is a reason for it:

> "You can't water a crop just once and expect it to survive." The secret: repeated doses of moisture, spread throughout the growing cycle. The same principle applies to learning. If we want learning to stick, we need to "water" it; we need to reinforce the learning multiple times . . . Research shows that retention is dramatically increased by what's called "interval reinforcement"—review or use of the material repeatedly over a period of time. If the brain registers information just once, less than 10 percent of the message is likely to be remembered after 30 days. But if there are six exposures to the information over 30 days, 90 percent of the message is likely to be retained.[23]

The apostles were about repetition. Paul said, "Do you not remember that while I was still with you, I was telling you these things" (2 Thess 2:5). Peter said, "This is now, beloved, the second letter I am writing to you in which I am stirring up your sincere mind by way of reminder, that you should remember the words spoken beforehand by the holy prophets and the commandment of the Lord and Savior spoken by your apostles" (2 Pet 3:1–2). One of the most vivid statements is in Romans 15:15: "But I have written very boldly to you on some points so as to remind you again, because of the grace that was given me from God." Paul had told them about some of those things before but felt it necessary to write them again. The writers of Scripture were constantly reminding the readers of their letters things that they had already been taught (see 2 Tim 2:14; Titus 3:1). Why was it necessary? For the same reason most preachers find it necessary to repeat themselves: Listeners forget. We do not listen intently the first time, for other things are more important to us. Therefore, preachers must repeat themselves often for our good.

---

23. Schultz and Schultz, *Dirt on Learning*, 79.

Second, be patient if our preachers are harsh. Harshness is not meant to be cruelty or meanness. Rather, it is saying the hard things that are difficult to hear. Once again, our preachers most likely have the best interests of their listeners at heart. Mark Driscoll, a preacher at Mars Hill Church in Seattle, has often said that hard words produce soft people and soft words produce hard people. When preachers say things that are hard to hear, they are trying to produce humility in their listeners and to soften their hearts. At some times, preachers will seem harsher than at others, maybe because of particular topics or texts. When this happens, keep in mind the longevity of their ministries. Remember the full scope of their preaching.

Third, be patient if our preachers are unclear. It is quite possible that they have had hard weeks. It is quite possible that every time they sat down to study, the phone rang and someone needed help. Maybe they were at the hospital all week. Maybe they did not get the preparation time that they needed that week. These are great opportunities to ask our pastors questions, to build those relationships with them we talked about in the last section. Just kindly go to them and ask, "What did you mean when you said_____?"

Fourth, be patient if our preachers are too long. The pot roast is probably already burnt. The restaurants are already filled. God's word is precious. How can it ever be too long?

Fifth, be patient if our preachers are too theological. This is why we need relationships with them, to talk with them about things like this. We can go to them and say something like this: "I was thinking about your sermon from Sunday. What are some practical ways that you have applied that theological truth to your life? What are some ways that I can apply it to my life?" I guarantee that if we approach our preachers with questions like that, they will be glad to answer them. In due time, they will be filling their sermons with those answers.

Why is it important for us to listen with patience? If we are not patient with our preachers, it will affect the way we listen to them preach. We will tune them out. We will miss important parts. We will miss argumentation. We will put words into the mouths of our preachers that they never said. Friends, let us listen patiently.

LISTEN HERMENEUTICALLY

Remember, discernment is the ability to examine and distinguish truth from error. The Bereans, in Acts 17, examined the Scriptures daily to see if what Paul was saying was true or false. To be a discerner of truth, we must study our Bibles. To listen hermeneutically means that we listen with an ear towards the set of rules used in interpreting the Bible accurately (hermeneutics). Most people have no idea how to study the Bible for themselves, which is probably the reason for so much error in the church today and so little discernment. If we have no desire to read and study God's word, it is very likely that we will not be on guard against false teaching. If we are not engaged in the Scriptures on a regular basis, discernment is going to be very tough, if it is possible at all. Get the point? The Bible needs to be read, but it also needs to be studied. One biblical scholar said,

> That God has spoken in Holy Scripture is the very heart of our faith and without this certainty we should be left to the relativity and dubiousness of human knowledge. God has spoken! But what has He said? This is the primary and basic need of hermeneutics: to ascertain what God has said in Sacred Scripture; to determine the meaning of the Word of God. There is no profit to us if God has spoken and we do not know what He has said. Therefore it is our responsibility to determine the meaning of what God has given to us in Sacred Scripture.[24]

This is of critical importance. If we have never taken a class on how to study the Bible, we should. If our churches do not offer such classes, we need to go to the pastors and ask if such classes can be taught. If our churches do not teach such classes, we can use one or more of several books to help us. The best book for the average person is *Living by the Book* by Dr. Howard Hendricks. Another helpful resource is by Gordon Fee, *How to Read the Bible for All Its Worth*. If we desire a deeper resource, the book Bernard Ramm wrote from which the previous quote was taken is somewhat of a classic in the field of hermeneutics.

Thabiti Anyabwile said, "Expositional preaching is that preaching which takes for the main point of a sermon the point of a particular passage of Scripture. If churches are to be healthy, then pastors and teachers must be committed to discovering the meaning of Scripture and allow-

---

24. Ramm, *Protestant Biblical Interpretation*, 1–2.

ing that meaning to drive the agenda with their congregations. There is an important corollary for every member of a local church. Just as the pastor's preaching agenda should be determined by the meaning of Scripture, so too should the Christian's listening agenda be driven by the meaning of Scripture."[25] This means that as we listen to the preaching of God's word, we should be concerned with discerning the truth of the intended meaning of a particular passage and its application to us today. To understand this fully, we must understand how to study the Bible.

The basic steps of Bible study are to (1) observe what the text says, (2) interpret what the text means, and then (3) apply the meaning to real life. Kent Hughes said, "You can never have a Christian mind without reading the Scriptures regularly because you cannot be profoundly influenced by that which you do not know."[26] Scripture reading is important, but Scripture studying is even more important. Although most people jump from observation to application without ever dealing with the hard work of interpretation, it is at the level of interpretation that real discernment happens. According to Adams, "Bible study is essential. If you are honest, you will admit that you don't study your Bible half enough. Maybe you don't study your Bible at all! I'm not talking about reading the Bible; if you want to become discerning, you must learn to study it. If you don't know the difference, or how to go about it, then it's time to learn. You must study your Bible because it is the Standard against which you must measure all teaching."[27]

MacArthur went even further, saying that the study of the Bible is the most important ingredient to become a discerner of truth: "All the desire in the world cannot make you discerning if you don't study Scripture. Prayer for discernment is not enough. Obedience alone will not suffice. Good role models won't do it either. Even the Holy Spirit will not give you discernment apart from His Word. If you really want to be discerning, you must diligently study the Word of God. God's Word is where you will learn the principles for discernment. It is there you will learn the truth. Only there can you follow the path of maturity."[28]

Why is it that everyone who talks about discernment eventually gets back to the issue of studying the Scriptures for ourselves? Is it be-

---

25. Anyabwile, *Healthy Church Member*, 19.
26. Hughes, *Disciplines of a Godly Man*, 77.
27. Adams, *Call for Discernment*, 86.
28. MacArthur, *Reckless Faith*, 87–88.

cause we will never have discernment without a good grasp of personal Bible study? If we want to be discerning, we must be persons of God's word. We must be absorbed with the Scriptures and know how to study them so that when we listen to sermons, we are in tune with interpreting Scripture. Friends, let us listen hermeneutically.

LISTEN HOMILETICALLY

Homiletics is often defined as the art of preaching. When we are attempting to discern preaching, it will be helpful if we understand how preaching works. There are at least four keys to unlocking the homiletics of a biblical sermon.

First, identify the principle thought. This is the main idea that the preacher is talking about in that particular sermon. It is called many different things: the central idea, the big idea, the theme, the subject, the sermon in a sentence, the dominating theme, and so on. Preachers should be able to summarize their sermons in a short sentence. Some preachers are very good at this; others struggle with it. As listeners, we should work hard at understanding the one major theme the preacher is talking about. We should have a good idea if the preacher keeps going back to support the one major theme.

We should be able to walk out of church knowing exactly what the preacher was saying. However, often we do not. It happens all the time. I have noticed when I preach on occasion that as I am standing by the door, some people will come and say that they really appreciated what I said and then will give some point of observation or application that is totally unrelated to what I preached. I am polite but am thinking, "That had nothing to do with what I was preaching on." I wondered if this was just happening to me, so I asked my preacher if this happens to him. He indicated that perhaps 30 percent of the comments he gets after each sermon have very little to do with the actual point of the sermon.

Second, identify the primary outline. Many preachers are outline oriented; some are not. If and when preachers give outlines, write them down. Outlines help reinforce the main thoughts in sermons.

Third, identify the purpose of the illustrations. The sermon is not about the illustrations. Yet, if we walk out of a sermon without understanding the point that the illustrations were intended to make, we have missed the point. To be effective listeners, we need to understand the points behind the illustrations. As the illustration is being offered, concentrate on the bridge that connects the illustration to the biblical principle. That way, the next day, it is not just some story but one with a theological point behind it.

Fourth, identify the practice of application. Discernment and listening to truth are not about filling heads with more information. We should be very careful that when we are listening, we are listening not only for the truth but also for the ways to apply that truth in our lives. Friends, let us listen homiletically.

LISTEN ACTIVELY

To listen actively means we are not passive. Rather, we are paying attention to bring something with us out of the sermon. One way to listen actively is to *take notes*. One of the first skills taught to college students is the skill of taking good notes. In *Note-Taking Made Easy*, the authors stated that taking notes helps a person pay attention, remember, and organize ideas.[29] These are all important when it comes to discernment. If we fail to pay attention, how will we know what the preacher says? If we fail to remember, how will we know what the preacher has said? If we fail to organize the ideas, how will we gain a flow of what was said? Take notes! They do not have to be extensive notes, but it is my feeling that everyone should walk out of the sermon with something.

The best use of notes is to review them. Summarize each page and then review them on Sunday afternoons or Monday mornings. This will greatly increase our abilities to know what was said and to remember it.

Another way to actively listen is to *prioritize the teaching*. Albert Mohler argued that all doctrine should be evaluated on three levels. The most important are the first level issues, "those doctrines most central and essential to the Christian faith."[30] They are the hinge pins on which the gospel and Christianity are hung. If any of them are removed, then we will fail to have biblical Christianity. What are the cardinal issues? He argued for doctrines such as the Trinity, the person and work of Jesus Christ, salvation by grace and faith alone, and the authority of Scriptures among others. Next are second level issues, doctrines that through disagreement "will create significant boundaries between believers."[31] These

---

29. Kesselman-Turkel and Peterson, *Note-Taking Made Easy*, 2–3.
30. Mohler, "Call for Theological Triage," lines 31–32.
31. Ibid., lines 59–60.

are issues that probably separate denominations while still being considered under the banner of orthodoxy. These may be the mode of baptism, some views of the Lord's Supper, or the miraculous gifts of the Spirit. Last are the third level issues, "doctrines over which Christians may disagree and remain in close fellowship, even within local congregations."[32] These may be issues such as the timing of the rapture and moderate drinking of alcohol.

In my estimation, this is critically important because if we are trying to examine and distinguish between right and wrong, we must know what hills to die on. In other words, we must know which issues are worth arguing or questioning and which are not. This will keep us listening actively because as we are thinking through the sermon, we need to determine what sort of issue we are trying to discern. In understanding different levels of importance, Mark Driscoll recommended that we list those things we would "die for, divide for, or debate for."[33] Wise individuals will approach their pastors over issues of death and division and will walk cautiously over those issues that are for debate. As one of my pastors used to say, nobody should shoot down flies with cannons. Friends, let us listen actively.

LISTEN LOVINGLY

This is the last point for a reason: The greatest temptation for those who love discernment issues is to examine truth outside of love. For some reason, there are some people who can smell error whenever it is within a thousand yards of their facilities. They are like drug dogs at an airport. For some, it is more about the truth and error than about the relationships with people. It is true that to discern truth from error is indeed a loving act. Some error attacks the roots of the gospel. Sniffing out that kind of error may mean the difference between eternal destruction and eternal life. Most people would have their arms cut off to save their lives, even though their arms may not seem to think they are being loved. In the same way, removing error from a body of believers or removing a teacher who is in its midst is something that the church is called to do. It is the best thing for the body of believers. Yet we must understand

---

32. Ibid., lines 79–80.
33. Driscoll and Breshears, *Vintage Church*, 158–59.

that it can be done in a loving manner, with an attitude of grace in the process.

The Apostle Paul said the mature person should be "speaking the truth in love" (Eph 4:15). Mature Christians are known for the truth, but the truth that comes from their mouths is said in a loving manner. In this context, there are some people who make it their objective to manipulate by trickery or to deceive people in religious circles. Paul said, the mature, equipped person is not that person. Doctrine does indeed matter, but it is just as important that the doctrine not become an intellectual exercise for the person without being encompassed with love.

"Speaking the truth in love" is a participle that may literally be read as "truthing it in love." This is not only about the way one talks but also about truth in doctrine and profession. Maturing believers are known as persons who are walking in a truthful way. It means both the speaking and the living of the truth, both of which are done in an attitude of love. Their message is not compromised by their lives and testimony and their lives and testimony are not compromised by their message. John Stott said,

> Thank God there are those in the contemporary church who are determined at all costs to defend and uphold God's revealed truth. But sometimes they are conspicuously lacking in love. When they think they smell heresy, their nose begins to twitch, their muscles ripple, and the light of battle enters their eye. They seem to enjoy nothing more than a fight. Others make the opposite mistake. They are determined at all costs to maintain and exhibit brotherly love, but in order to do so are prepared even to sacrifice the central truths of revelation. Both these tendencies are unbalanced and unbiblical. Truth becomes hard if it is not softened by love; love becomes soft if it is not strengthened by truth.[34]

What Stott was saying is that truth and love are to go hand in hand. Individuals' actions are going to display how much they care for truth and how much they care about love. Their love is to temper the truth, and the truth is to firm their love.

As we listen to sermons, there are two extremes that we should avoid. The first extreme is *cold-hearted arrogance*. This is the arrogance that says these individuals are always right and everyone else is always wrong. This mindset is prevalent in those ministries that stress discern-

---

34. Stott, *Message of Ephesians*, 172.

ment. In speaking of one of the dangers of discernment, Tim Challies made this observation: "Those who witch hunt end up riding brooms. Sooner or later, Christians who spend their days seeking out and responding to the transgressions of other people can quickly become insufferable. The spiritual oppression inherent in continually seeking out what is evil begins to take its toll. Their attempts in discernment somehow lead them to forsake discernment."[35]

Unfortunately, this happens all the time. I have seen it happen with my own eyes. I have friends who emphasize discernment to such a degree that eventually people turn on them, claiming they are just using discernment. Once again, go back to that list of priorities in the last section. What should a person be willing to die for? I often joke with some people that there are some truths I will die for and some that I will not even give a friend's right arm for. Cold-hearted, arrogant people unknowingly stress discernment without love and eventually see every issue as the most important issue. These people are ungracious with others.

Love balances truth. When they are out of balance, there is trouble. How do we know if they are out of balance in us? Do we always focus on the negative? Do we always seem to point out the wrong in others but never encourage them when they are right? Are we quick to point out faults but not praise successes? If so, we are probably out of balance. One good way for me to evaluate my heart is to ask my children. Do my children think of me as the swift ruler of rules or the one graciously recognizing when they obey the rules? Children need encouragement when they obey, not just discipline when they fail to obey.

Are we tempted to be critical of how other Christians are living, what they are reading, how they are spending their time? Recently, I returned from lunch with a man who just berated our church and leadership. Everything was negative, nothing positive. There was probably—no, certainly—some truth behind what he was saying, but the manner in which he said it made me want never to have lunch with him again. His truth was far from tempered with love: "The tongue of the wise makes knowledge acceptable, but the mouth of fools spouts folly" (Prov 15:2).

The worst group of people who focus on the negative and tend to be harsh are first-year Bible college students. They go away, come home, and magically are experts in everything, as if they took some magic pill in one year: The preacher is unbiblical, his sermons are not accurate, the

---

35. Challies, *Discipline of Spiritual Discernment*, 146–47.

music is not theological, and people are missing in fellowship. They are tempted to be extremely arrogant without showing any form of love. I say this because I know. I lived it!

Do those we disagree with know we love them? Do our neighbors who disagree with our view of salvation know that we will still mow their lawns? When error arises, do we do everything we can to let the people in error know that we care for them? Will we serve them? Will we help them move? This is where the rub comes. If we approach our pastors about something that we believe to be unbiblical in their sermons, will they know that we care for them, that we love them?

Do we talk more than we listen? Those who seem to emphasize truth over love tend to talk more and listen less; those who emphasize love over truth seem to listen more and talk less. Much of what is assumed to be error in the sermon can be attributed to a person talking too much and listening too little. James said, "Everyone must be quick to hear, slow to speak and slow to anger" (Jas 1:19). The Lord gave two ears and one mouth; there is probably a reason for that. Maybe by restraining the lips and using the ears instead of the mouth, a person can avoid the problems of cold-hearted arrogance.

The other extreme is *warm-hearted ignorance*. There are those who think they can simply love without truth: "If I simply love someone enough, they will soon obey God." This is the mom who wants her daughter to be happy and so does not want to be confrontational about her sleeping with her boyfriend. Maybe if she just supports and loves her enough, there will be a window open to discuss things. That is simply ludicrous. "We've redefined Christlike to mean 'nice.' By that definition, Christ wasn't always Christlike. He confronted people with sin, raised His voice, threw tables, and called people snakes, blind hypocrites, and white-washed tombs. If we don't talk about sin and hell because we want to be nice, we're trying to be nicer than Jesus, who spoke a great deal about both."[36]

This is just one of the errors that plague the emergent church in today's culture. These people love the thought of reaching others but fear offending them. This fear strangles them so much that they change their message to reach others. Do we avoid conflict at all costs? They avoid confrontation because they know it will be difficult, but sometimes con-

---

36. Alcorn, *Grace and Truth Paradox*, 73.

flict is unavoidable. Conflict is often necessary to bring a person back onto the right path.

My oldest son has really long eyelashes, the kind that many women spend lots of money to get. A few times in his life, he has been hit in the face and his eyelashes have turned inside out so that they are on his eyeball. Extreme pain! To see the problem, he has to open his eye, even though that will make the problem worse. We have to make him do it because that is what is best for him. I do not just sit there, hug him, and say that it will be okay someday. Yet some people are like that. They just want to hug or love on others and not deal with what really needs to be done. Jesus confronted people and told them things that they did not want to hear, but that was what they needed.

Do we care more for people or for the Lord? Does our love of Jesus far outweigh our love for others? For some people, the thought of confrontation paralyzes them because they care more for what other persons say than for what Jesus says. If Jesus says he is the only way anyone can get to heaven, then that truth should go forth no matter how much it may offend the other person.

It does not matter if we struggle with cold-hearted arrogance or warm-hearted ignorance. If we are out of balance, then we will be in trouble. Both of these can be damaging to the church and the pursuit of truth. Randy Alcorn adequately summarized the issue:

> Truth-oriented Christians love studying Scripture and theology. But sometimes they're quick to judge and slow to forgive. They're strong on truth, weak on grace. Grace-oriented Christians love forgiveness and freedom. But sometimes they neglect Bible study and see moral standards as "legalism." They're strong on grace, weak on truth. Countless mistakes in marriage, parenting, ministry, and other relationships are failures to balance grace and truth. Sometimes we neglect both. Often we choose one over the other ... Truth without grace breeds a self-righteous legalism that poisons the church and pushes the world away from Christ. Grace without truth breeds moral indifference and keeps people from seeing their need for Christ. Attempts to "soften" the gospel by minimizing truth keep people from Jesus. Attempts to "toughen" the gospel by minimizing grace keep people from Jesus. It's not enough for us to offer grace or truth. We must offer both.[37]

---

37. Ibid., 17–18.

Examine the Preaching of God's Word 99

When we examine the preaching of God's word, it is possible to do it with love. We should check our attitudes to see if our motivation is only to point out error to boost our pride. We should care not only for the truth but also for the person. Friends, let us listen lovingly.

It was stated earlier in this chapter that after Paul left Thessalonica, he went to Berea and found them to be more "noble-minded than those in Thessalonica" (Acts 17:11). Paul then wrote back to the church at Thessalonica and told them to "examine everything carefully; hold fast to that which is good; abstain from every form of evil" (1 Thess 5:21–22). Once truth has been examined and found to be true or not, there is an appropriate response. That is what the next chapter is about: what people are to do once they have examined the truth of God's word preached.

4

Live the Preaching of God's Word

A FEW YEARS AGO, while reading a book on spiritual leadership, I was moved to the point of anger by one of the most famous pastors in America. Towards the beginning of the book, he was trying to chronicle the secret ingredient to successful, thriving churches. He talked about the ineffectiveness of location and denominational support, and then he wrote one paragraph that literally stopped me. I did a double take and gave some serious thought to our church and churches like ours. He said,

> Maybe the key to thriving churches is great preaching. But I didn't have to look any further than the United States to debunk that theory. Although many preaching-centered churches attract large crowds, their impact on the community is often negligible. The church is packed for an hour on Sunday, but empty during the week. *Sermon junkies tend to stay in their comfortable pews, growing ever more knowledgeable while becoming ever less involved in the surrounding community.* Conversions are rare because there's little outreach . . . The body is being fed and satisfied in a corporate teaching setting, but that's about all that's happening.[1]

I remember sitting there, arguing with him in my head that the preaching and teaching of God's word have to be central and powerful keys to effective churches. However, as I reflected on what he said, I determined that the issue is not that preaching-centered churches are ineffective. The problem is that the preaching or teaching produces no action in the lives of the people.

I hope that all churches that emphasize the preaching of God's word produce more than just sermon junkies only looking for their next fix of truth. I agree with Hybels in this regard, if preaching and teaching

---

1. Hybels, *Courageous Leadership*, 25. Emphasis mine.

only produce people sitting in their pews, never acting upon the truth, then there is little point to that truth. I disagree with him in this regard: I believe the key to thriving churches is hearing a word from God through the preaching of his word, but the word has not been listened to if people do not do something with it. As I have thought about this issue, maybe the problem is not preaching churches but listeners who are not really listening. They have failed to live the preaching of God's word.

We said at the beginning of this book that to talk about listening to the preaching of God's word without emphasizing its application is ridiculous. The assumption we have been making all along that will be clarified in this chapter is that biblical listening does not happen if God's word does not make a difference in the lives of the persons who listen. This certainly was not true of the church in Thessalonica. They lived the preaching of God's word.

In many ways, the church at Thessalonica is a great teacher for us in how to listen to the preaching of God's word; for we have a chronicle of their good habits and their bad. They received the word of God preached to them by Paul, which means they were prepared to give it an audience. They did not examine it as they should have, as the people of Berea did who examined the Scriptures daily to see whether what Paul was saying was accurate or not. When writing back to the Thessalonians, Paul exhorted them to do a better job of examining the teaching of God's word in the future. If they found it to be false, they were to reject it; but if they found it to be true, they were to hold onto it. This leads to the third step in the process of biblical listening: There is no biblical listening to preaching if we do not live the preaching of God's word.

The Thessalonians were a people of action. They lived the word of God preached. Paul commended them at the beginning of his first letter that the "gospel did not come to you in word only, but also in power and in the Holy Spirit and with full conviction; just as you know what kind of men we proved to be among you for your sake. You also became imitators of us and of the Lord, having received the word in much tribulation with the joy of the Holy Spirit, so that you became an example to all the believers in Macedonia and in Achaia" (1 Thess 1:5–7).

They accepted the gospel amidst major persecution, which led to what? They became examples to all the believers in Macedonia and in Achaia. Obviously, they lived some of the preached word that they heard. Paul then continued to show them how to live the word of God preached: "For the word of the Lord has sounded forth from you, not only in Macedonia and Achaia, but also in every place your faith toward God has gone forth, so that we have no need to say anything. For they themselves report about us what kind of a reception we had with you, and how you turned to God from idols to serve a living and true God, and to wait for His Son from heaven, whom He raised from the dead, that is Jesus, who rescues us from the wrath to come" (1 Thess 1:8–10). Their response to the preaching of God's word was like a sonic boom in their community. These people were known for their response to the sermons. They were not sermon junkies who were only there for information; they changed drastically. They repented of their idols, turned to God, and waited for his son in worship.

Why do we not see this sort of result from the preaching of God's word today? Why do our states not know about the responses of our churches in our cities? I think it is because we have tricked ourselves into thinking that we are good listeners to preaching even though we do not change our lives when we hear that preaching. How can we live the preaching of God's word? That is what the rest of this chapter is about, points of response to living God's word preached.

RESPOND WITH FAITH

Living any preaching of God's word begins with our faith. It starts with us believing something. When Paul told the people of Thessalonica to "hold fast to that which is good; abstain from every form of evil" (1 Thess 5:21–22), he meant that if they found the teaching to be true, they were to make it part of their lives. Another way to say this is given in 1 Thessalonians 2:13 when Paul commended them: "For this reason we also constantly thank God that when you received the word of God which you heard from us, you accepted it not as the word of men, but for what it really is, the word of God, which also performs its work in you who believe." Notice that not only did they receive the word of God but also accepted it. On the surface, it may seem that Paul was saying the same thing; but there is a slight difference between receiving and accepting the word preached. "When you *received* (external reception) from us 'the word of hearing' (meaning: the word which you heard), which was nothing less than God's own word, you *accepted* (inward welcoming) it *as such*, that is, as a word of God and not as a word of men."[2] At what point do people internalize a message and make it their own? It is at the point of faith. It is at the point that they believe the message.

There is a very clear distinction that needs to be made at this point. As Christians, we often see faith as a means to enter into a relationship with Jesus Christ. We believe what he says about himself. We believe what he has done for us. We believe and trust him to save us from our sins. But then we forget about the issue of faith. We need to understand that faith and action in obedience must be hand in hand. If we walk out of any sermon and try to obey that sermon apart from faith, we are living a works-based religion. Our obedience begins with faith; and, in reality, our obedience is an act of faith. Let me see if I can explain this biblically.

The Apostle Paul at the beginning of Romans argued that he was called to be an apostle for the gospel of God: "Jesus Christ our Lord, through whom we have received grace and apostleship to bring about *the obedience of faith* among all the Gentiles for His name's sake" (Rom 1:4–5, emphasis mine). Paul then concluded the book with a similar statement. "Now to Him who is able to establish you according to my gospel and the preaching of Jesus Christ, according to the revelation of the mystery which has been kept secret for long ages past, but now is manifested, and by the Scriptures of the prophets, according to the commandment of the eternal God, has been made known to all the nations, leading *to obedience of faith*; to the only wise God, through Jesus Christ, be the glory forever. Amen" (Rom 16:25–27, emphasis mine). What does Paul mean by "the obedience of faith?" Is it that obedience arises from faith or is it that faith is in itself obedience? One of the leading scholars on the book of Romans, Douglas Moo, summarized Paul's statement in this way:

> Paul saw his task as calling men and women to submission to the lordship of Christ (cf., vv. 4b and 7b), a submission that began with conversion but which was to continue in a deepening, lifelong commitment. This obedience to Christ as Lord is always closely related to faith, both as an initial, decisive step of faith and as a continuing "faith" relationship with Christ. In light of this, we understand the words "obedience" and "faith" to be mutually interpreting: obedience always involves faith, and faith always in-

---

2. Hendriksen and Kistemaker, *Thessalonians*, 69.

volves obedience. They should not be equated, compartmentalized, or made into separate stages of Christian experience. Paul called men and women to a faith that was always inseparable from obedience—for the Savior in whom we believe is nothing less than our Lord—and to an obedience that could never be divorced from faith—for we can obey Jesus as Lord only when we have given ourselves to him in faith.[3]

What he means is that we should be careful of dividing faith and obedience from each other too drastically. Maybe it is both. Maybe when we talk about obedience, we should be talking about faith. Maybe when we are talking about faith, we should be talking about the obedience that follows. Faith is what is needed as the entrance, but it is also needed as the key ingredient throughout the Christian life. James said that any faith that does not produce actions is useless faith, a faith that does not save (Jas 2:14–26). We cannot have obedience without faith, and we cannot have faith without obedience.

How does this make a difference in listening to preaching? When something is said from the pulpit, we then take that and examine it against the Scriptures to see if it is true or not. If it is found to be from God, are we ready by faith to take the actions required by that sermon? Paul said that the word of God does indeed perform its work but only in those who believe (1 Thess 2:13). We cannot ever respond accurately to a sermon if we do not believe in the truth that is being promoted. Let me explain this in two ways, one biblically and one illustratively.

First, biblically, what is it that the writer of Hebrews said helps us to "lay aside every encumbrance and the sin which so easily entangles us" and "run with endurance the race that is set before us" (Heb 12:1)? For certain, it is "fixing our eyes on Jesus, the author and perfecter [sic] of faith" (Heb 12:2); but it is also the cloud of witnesses that surrounds us, standing on the shore of the great stadium, cheering us on in our walks with Jesus in this Christian life. They are those who have successfully run the race of the Christian life by faith.

Hebrews 11 has long been described as the hall of faith. A quick observance of the people in this great chapter shows us that faith was not something that they just did before being saved. It was what allowed them to do anything throughout life for the Lord. Each account is a characterization of a man or woman who obeyed what the Lord told

---

3. Moo, *Epistle to the Romans*, 52–53.

the person to do, even though everything earthly called the individual stupid for doing so. That is what faith is all about. It is "the assurance of things hoped for, the conviction of things not seen" (Heb 11:1). They each followed God's word and believed that he would take care of them if they did what they were told to do.

Take, for instance, Noah: "By faith Noah, being warned by God about things not yet seen, in reverence prepared an ark for the salvation of his household, by which he condemned the world, and became an heir of the righteousness which is according to faith" (Heb 11:7). We should put ourselves in Noah's situation. It has never rained on the face of the earth. In fact, the thought of rain is foreign to every person there. I can imagine Noah in that conversation with God: "Okay, so you are saying that you are bringing a flood of water upon the earth, so like water coming from the heavens and water from underneath the earth? Okay? That has never happened before on the face of the earth, but I believe you that it will happen." We have no idea what it was like for Noah to build an ark to protect from a level of water that had never been seen. We have no idea what it was like for Noah to preach about what was going to happen to a group of people who ridiculed and mocked him every day. What was it that moved Noah to obey God and do these things? It was his faith that God had something greater than earthly relationships and friendships. It was his faith in God that he was a "rewarder of those who seek Him" (Heb 11:6).

Take, for instance, Abraham. What was it that moved him to pick up his household and leave everything that he had ever known for a land that he had never seen before (Heb 11:8–10)? What was it, after he had been promised that he would receive an inheritance and that his family would be like the sand on the seashore through his son Isaac, that made him willing to kill that son (Heb 11:17–19)? Abraham believed that God is faithful to his promises. Because his promises were to come through Isaac, even though God was now telling him to kill his son, Abraham knew God was going to do something amazing: "He considered that God is able to raise people even from the dead" (Heb 11:19). His faith was active and living all throughout his life, and it moved him into actions of obedience.

Take, for instance, Moses. We may need to learn the faith of Moses more than any other character in the Scriptures. What is it that moves someone to choose "rather to endure ill-treatment with the people of

God than to enjoy the passing pleasures of sin, considering the reproach of Christ greater riches than the treasures of Egypt" (Heb 11:25–26)? It is faith in God that his eternal ways are more enjoyable than the temporal ways of the world. Imagine being in Egypt and God coming to you and saying, "I want you kill a lamb and paint the door of your house with the blood or else I will come and kill the firstborn son in the night." Hmm, okay. Seems a little strange. Yet Moses, by faith, "kept the Passover and the sprinkling of the blood, so that he who destroyed the firstborn would not touch them" (Heb 11:28).

Get the point? Whether Noah, Abraham, Moses, or any of the other people mentioned in Hebrews 11, their faith moved them to obey. It is this issue of faith that will make or break our listening to preaching. Friends, be warned. Read with caution this strong warning that centers on the issue of our heart of faith:

> Therefore, just as the Holy Spirit says, "TODAY IF YOU HEAR HIS VOICE, DO NOT HARDEN YOUR HEARTS AS WHEN THEY PROVOKED ME, AS IN THE DAY OF TRIAL IN THE WILDERNESS, WHERE YOUR FATHERS TRIED ME BY TESTING ME, AND SAW MY WORKS FOR FORTY YEARS. "THEREFORE I WAS ANGRY WITH THIS GENERATION, AND SAID, 'THEY ALWAYS GO ASTRAY IN THEIR HEART, AND THEY DID NOT KNOW MY WAYS'; AS I SWORE IN MY WRATH, 'THEY SHALL NOT ENTER MY REST.'" *Take care, brethren, that there not be in any one of you an evil, unbelieving heart that falls away from the living God.* But encourage one another day after day, as long as it is still called "Today," so that none of you will be hardened by the deceitfulness of sin. For we have become partakers of Christ, if we hold fast the beginning of our assurance firm until the end, while it is said, "TODAY IF YOU HEAR HIS VOICE, DO NOT HARDEN YOUR HEARTS, AS WHEN THEY PROVOKED ME." For who provoked Him when they had heard? Indeed, did not all those who came out of Egypt led by Moses? And with whom was He angry for forty years? Was it not with those who sinned, whose bodies fell in the wilderness? And to whom did He swear that they would not enter His rest, but to those who were disobedient? So we see that they were not able to enter because of unbelief. (Heb 3:7–19, emphasis mine)

Two times he said, "Today if you hear his voice . . . do not harden your hearts." Then, in verse 13, he warned against the hardening of the hearts because of sin. He said it again in Hebrews 4:7, a warning against hardening our hearts and listening to God's voice. Most of this passage is a quote from Psalm 95:7–8 in which the psalmist tells the people that they are not to be like their fathers in the wilderness where they constantly failed to listen to God and their hearts became hardened. The reason for not listening is seen in the warning in verse 12: "Take care, brethren, that there not be in any one of you an evil, unbelieving heart that falls away from the living God."

The hard heart is a result of unbelief: "The greatest sin in the world is unbelief. It is the greatest offense against God and brings the greatest harm to ourselves."[4] It is a subtle shift, for people never just fall off cliffs. They take little step after little step, moving closer and closer to the edge. Persons who become hardened to the things of God start with little compromises in which they do not believe God. Those lead to greater compromises.

Where do we stand in listening to preaching? If we continually walk out of preaching and never have the faith actually to apply what is being taught, we are slowly and slowly hardening our hearts to the word of the Lord. Someday we may wake up and be characterized as having "evil, unbelieving heart[s]." I do not want that for any of us. The only way to fight that is to make certain that we respond with faith to the preaching of God's word every time we listen to it preached. We must choose to live our lives by faith.

But how is this practically seen in our lives? What is it that allows any of us to leave our sin? Imagine a person has been stealing at work. On Sunday at church, the message happens to be on Ephesians 4:28, which says, "He who steals must steal no longer." The pastor admonishes the people in the audience that if they have stolen, they need to make it right and make recompense for their actions. What is going to move the person sitting in the audience who has stolen to confess to the boss? The person knows the boss will most certainly terminate the individual. Then the person will have a hard time finding a new job to take care of the family because of the tough economy. What will move such a person to obey? It is the belief that the Lord is the one who will provide and take care of the person's family. It is the belief that the Lord is the rewarder of those who live their lives in obedience to Him. It is the person's faith.

---

4. MacArthur, *Hebrews*, 92.

Imagine another scenario in which a wife is lying to her husband concerning finances. Maybe she has kept some credit cards from him and has racked up some serious debt. One Sunday at church, her pastor preaches on Colossians 3:9, which says, "Do not lie to one another, since you laid aside the old self with its evil practices." She leaves the service under heavy conviction to tell her husband how she has been lying to him over the past couple of years. She knows that if she tells him, his temper and anger will ignite and life will be nothing short of hell on earth. She knows that she can hide it and everything will remain as it is, yet she knows she is disobeying the Lord. What is it that is going to move her to tell him and risk upsetting her husband and facing a tormented life? It is her faith that Jesus means more than anything else in this world. Now imagine that she does tell her husband. At that moment, he is faced with forgiveness. What will move him to forgive instead of making her life miserable? It is faith that the Lord is the avenger and that his reputation is found in Jesus, not in himself.

This issue of faith is everything. We can look at every sin and come to the same result. Do we really believe what the Lord says is more important than our own comfortable situations in life? Do we really believe that if we obey God and do what he has told us to do, our lives will be better, even if it means that the external parts of our lives will be worse? We all need faith every single day of our lives. We will never respond to the preaching of God's word if we do not cultivate hearts of faith every single day. Friends, let us respond with faith.

RESPOND WITH THOUGHTFULNESS

Authentic Christians should have authentic responses to the words of Jesus Christ. We know this from Jesus himself. One of the most well-known parables given by Jesus comes at the end of the most famous sermon he ever preached. Jesus had been traveling throughout the region of Galilee (the north end of Israel), performing many miracles and taking many opportunities to teach the crowds concerning the kingdom of heaven. He had just called his twelve men, the men that he would disciple and use to change the world. These men were with him now on a twenty-four hour basis. They abandoned their jobs and families and committed themselves to come and be with Jesus. They believed that Jesus is the Messiah, the chosen one to deliver the nation of Israel from its oppression. They knew the Old Testament and were probably anticipating Christ starting his kingdom on the earth right then and there with them as his apprentices. As Jesus ministered, it was apparent that more and more people were beginning to follow him. They were intrigued that he was a great miracle worker. They were fascinated by how he stood up to the regimented rules of the Pharisees, particularly in regard to the man-made rules concerning the Sabbath. For many of them, he was the show that had to be attended. Matthew records, "When Jesus saw the crowds, He went up on the mountain; and after He sat down, His disciples came to Him. He opened His mouth and began to teach them, saying," (Matt 5:1–2).

What follows is known as the Sermon on the Mount. It is very important to understand that Matthew 5–7 is a sermon by Jesus. In the sermon, Jesus took the law and expanded it from the external to the internal. He dealt specifically with the hearts of his people. Towards the end of the sermon, Jesus specifically declared there are only two possible teams to play on, his team and the opposite team. In Matthew 7:13–14, Jesus said there are only two gates, two roads, and two destinations. He then said that there are only two trees, two types of fruit, and two destinations. Then he said that there will be many on the day of judgment who will say to him, "Lord, Lord . . . look at what we have done" and he will say to them, "Depart from Me." But he did say that the ones who will enter are the ones who do "the will of My Father who is in heaven" (Matt 7:21–23). This, in turn, led into his grand conclusion to the greatest sermon ever preached:

> "Therefore everyone who hears these words of Mine and acts on them, may be compared to a wise man who built his house on the rock. And the rain fell, and the floods came, and the winds blew and slammed against that house; and yet it did not fall, for it had been founded on the rock. Everyone who hears these words of Mine and does not act on them, will be like a foolish man who built his house on the sand. The rain fell, and the floods came, and the winds blew and slammed against that house; and it fell— and great was its fall." When Jesus had finished these words, the crowds were amazed at His teaching; for He was teaching them as one having authority, and not as their scribes. (Matt. 7:24–29)

Please note that this parable about the wise man and the foolish man comes immediately after a statement of who will enter the kingdom and who will be rejected. The only distinction between these two fellows is that one of them "hears the words and acts on them." Jesus was not teaching some sort of works-based salvation; for continually throughout the Sermon on the Mount, he said that a person would have to be perfect to enter the Kingdom. His conclusion is his final appeal. Are we going to obey and listen and be different based upon what we hear in his sermon or not?

The story in the previous parable is rather simple. It can be summarized as one man who was hasty and one who was thoughtful. One man builds a house on the rock, and another man builds a house on the sand. When the rains, wind, and storms come, the house built on the rock stands firm. The house built on the sand crumbles. Why? Because there is no foundation. The foolish man had built his house on shallow ground. The foundation is the only difference between these two builders. It is presumably the same house built in the same area, for they are hit by the same storm.

The Jews would have understood this sort of building and this sort of situation. It was not uncommon in their area for the climate to be calm during the dry season. But the wet season could come on in a flash. When storms arose suddenly, flash floods were created. During such floods, the wind blew and houses were slammed with waves and wind. It was during these times that the foundations of the houses meant everything. The wise man responded thoughtfully because he knew that the dry season was not going to last forever. He worked hard during the dry season in preparation for the wet season. He worked hard up front to ensure that his results were long lasting.

Our responses to the words of Jesus need to be carefully thought out because we are looking for real life changes, not just quick fixes. We do not want to be the soil of the rocky place as Jesus later explained: "The man who hears the word and immediately receives it with joy; yet he has no firm root in himself, but is only temporary, and when affliction or persecution arises because of the word, immediately he falls away" (Matt 13:20–21). Sometimes deep-rooted sins and issues in our lives will be hard to deal with in a minute, a day, or even a week. However, repentance can and should happen immediately, even though the fruit of the repentance may take a long time to appear.

Let's take this one step further. In the corresponding passage of the two builders, Luke recorded that the man who built on the rock "*dug deep* and laid a foundation on the rock." (Luke 6:48, emphasis mine). The wise man had to work hard to build his house; the foolish man did not work hard at all. It was easy for him. He was comfortable with shallow responses to the Lord's words.

As I write this, our church is engaged in a small building project. We are on the third week of a seven-week project. The contractors are just starting to do work above ground. There has been a lot of labor, time, money, and energy spent on what is unseen. It would have been cheaper, quicker, and easier to do the project without a foundation; but it would have been foolish. To live the preaching of the word of God will take hard work and some thoughtfulness because it is not an easy message. The wise builder measured, remeasured, and probably ran to Home Depot several times. It took lots of work. A. W. Pink pointedly explained why hard work is needed when it comes to applying the words of Jesus:

> Among the sayings of Christ are some peculiarly distasteful to flesh and blood, yea, at direct variance with the inclinations of fallen human nature. To pluck out right eyes and cut off right hands, to love our enemies, bless them which curse us, do good to them that hate us, and pray for them which despitefully use and persecute us, is not so simple as it may sound—see, then, the appropriateness of our Lord's similitude of digging deep when portraying such tasks. To distribute our alms and perform our devotions in secret, to expressly ask the Father to forgive us our debts as we forgive our debtors—being told that if we forgive not neither shall we be forgiven—to take no anxious thought for the morrow but to have a heart freed from carking care, to have such confidence in the providential bounty of God that we trustfully count upon Him supplying our every need, are duties which will tax our abilities to the utmost. True, but we shall not be the losers by practicing *[sic]* such precepts.[5]

Responding to the words of the sermon demand thoughtfulness because we must count the cost (Luke 14:28–31). This means that if we walk out of church from listening to the preaching of God's word and dismiss it, forget about it, and not think deeply about it, we are missing the point. Or if we walk out of church and the application of the truth is easy for us, we may be choosing the easy way over the hard way. We really need to deal with that. How have we worked hard at applying the truth that our preacher preached this past Sunday? Have we dug deep?

---

5. Pink, *Exposition*, 430.

There is one other passage that helps us understand what it means to respond thoughtfully to the preaching of God's word. As with the illustration of Jesus, his brother James gave us a word picture we can easily understand. He may have been recounting a story that Jesus had told. "But prove yourselves doers of the word, and not merely hearers who delude themselves. For if anyone is a hearer of the word and not a doer, he is like a man who looks at his natural face in a mirror; for once he has looked at himself and gone away, he has immediately forgotten what kind of person he was. But one who looks intently at the perfect law, the law of liberty, and abides by it, not having become a forgetful hearer but an effectual doer, this man will be blessed in what he does" (Jas 1:22–25).

James said that on one side are the hearers of the word of God. They are the ones who come and sit and listen to the preaching of God's word. They may even take notes. They sit there, they do their duty, and they are faithful. They are committed to the word of God being preached. They may even say amen a few times. But they fail to act upon the sermon being preached. The other group he described as the doers of the word of God. These are the ones who also hear the word preached. They also come to church, sit, and listen to the word preached. They probably take notes as well. They are faithful to what the Lord would have them do during this time, but the difference is that they walk out of the sermon and are different. This is our goal, to be doers of the truth.

Homer Kent observed that James tells them not to "do the word" but to be "doers of the word."[6] One reason our living of the preaching of God's word requires thoughtfulness is that it is something we are to be, not just something we are to do. If we are told to "do the word," then it becomes works of obedience. It is merely duty. It would be easy for us to say, "Give me the list and watch me work my way down the list" or "Pastor, give me the three points of application and I can do it." No, what is being said is that we need to become "doers of the word." The distinction is wrapped up in the heart of the issue. It is not a list of things the person does; it is who the person is. Doers of the word pattern their lives after the things of God. When they see things they are struggling in, they quickly deal with those issues.

Those who are hearers only delude themselves. How have they deceived themselves? They do so in thinking that listening to informa-

---

6. Kent, *Faith That Works*, 65.

tion is the end goal of the Christian life, of their own personal godliness: "Many still determine their godliness by the quality of hearing (for instance sermons) or reading (even God's word) instead of action and obedience."[7]

The illustration used by James is somewhat humorous. The person woke up in the morning and looked at himself in the mirror. The image was seen and noticed (not a mere glance, but a look). The person saw the imperfections of his hair or skin or whatever. Then the person left the mirror and immediately forgot what he looked like. I understand that some of us may wish to leave the mirror and forget what we look like, but nobody really does that. We remember the imperfections we have. The point of this illustration is that the time in front of the mirror for this man was wasted. Why did he even look at himself in the mirror if he was going to leave and forget? That's the point. The time standing before the mirror was a waste of time. In the same way, people who sit under the preaching of God's word, leave, and fail to heed, change, or be impacted by that word have wasted their time.

Can you imagine that? We give the word an audience by coming prepared. We examine it according to what the Scriptures have said to see if it is true. But if we stop there without ever responding thoughtfully to the preached word, according to James, everything we have done prior to this is a waste of our time. Is it a waste of time because the word is not powerful enough? No, it is a waste of our time because we do not accomplish what the word has been designed for, to change us. If we fail to be doers of the word, we are hearers only, or as Jesus said, foolish builders.

So many times, we sit in the audience waiting for God to do the big things in our lives. We wait for those home-run sermons from our preachers when everything seems to click perfectly and we walk out on cloud nine, our lives radically different. In reality, those times are very infrequent. Our responses to sermons should be evaluated more in terms of single sermons. You know, those infield-single sermons that barely make it back to the pitcher. It is in those sermons that we prove ourselves to be doers of the word. They may not be sermons that rock our world; but if they are truth, there is something in them that needs to make us think about something in our lives. We should walk out being different.

---

7. Hiebert, *James*, 119.

Thinking of that overwhelms me. Responding thoughtfully should mean to us that there is something in every sermon for us to work on. I often advise people just to ponder one thing after the sermon about their lives and work just on that one thing. We should not try to change everything about our lives but focus on just one thing at a time. Take a baby step. Then next week, take another baby step, then one more, and so on.

Why should we respond thoughtfully? According to James, those persons who look at the perfect law and abide by it will be blessed. Note that blessing does not happen to the hearers, to those who are coming to church to hear the sermon. The blessing comes to those who abide by the Scriptures. When we abide by the word of God preached, we are blessed.

Jesus says we are wise and the other Scriptures affirm this reality. David said that in keeping the Scriptures "there is great reward" (Ps 19:11). The consistent testimony of the Scriptures is that blessings follow those who hear the word of God and obey it. What is the blessing? This is where western Christianity has really messed things up. It is not that everything always turns out perfectly. It does not mean that our wives will never leave us, that our businesses will always thrive, and that our children will become perfectly obedient. It does not mean, as some say, that our lives will be perfectly happy, earthly speaking. Certainly part of the blessing is knowing that we are obeying our Lord and Savior Jesus Christ, but it is also a deep-rooted inner joy that the world knows nothing about. It is eternal in nature, not temporal. As we are hard at work applying the sermons to ourselves, we are building for ourselves eternal treasures that are not necessarily seen upon this earth. Friends, let us respond with thoughtfulness.

RESPOND WITH SPECIFICS

A biblical response to God's truth will change us in terms of having more Christ-like character. One of the ways that James indicates this happens is that the truth of Scripture should make us deal with specific issues in our lives. "If anyone thinks himself to be religious, and yet does not bridle his tongue but deceives his own heart, this man's religion is worthless. Pure and undefiled religion in the sight of our God and Father is this: to visit orphans and widows in their distress, and to keep oneself unstained by the world" (Jas 1:26–27).

Many commentators split these verses from the previous section, stating that James moved onto a new thought, describing what real religion is all about. I think they are mistaken. On the surface, verses 22–25 and verse 26 seem to contradict each other. Just before, James said that we should not be hearers only but doers. Then he condemned those who are doing. Why? Because the Spirit of God knows human nature. He knows that our temptation is to jump in and do and do and do things. It does not matter how much we do if we are not changed internally. This is the connection to the Scriptures; we need to change internally so that externally we joyfully engage in pursuits of thankfulness to Jesus, not in dutiful deeds of religion.

How do we know if we are changing? How can we know if we are living the truth of God's word? We need to ask ourselves these questions. *First, how does this truth help me control that which controls me?* James first talked about the issue of self-control, proposing a hypothetical situation. Imagine someone who does the external acts of religion. He attends worship services, observes the ordinances, and serves in the junior high department. He fasts, prays, gives to the building fund, memorizes Scripture, takes his kids to church, sings in the choir, and so on: He does the religious things. This looks normal, but this may be a dangerous place for one to be. Yes, these are all things we thing we should be doing; but James said that he "thinks" himself to be religious. People who think that performing acts of religion fulfills some sort of religious obligation are in trouble. We can be the greatest servants, give the most money, share the most of our time, and do all things religious; but if we do not bridle our tongues, we are deceived. Our religion is worthless.

Why is the tongue the standard? The tongue is used as an example of any part of the body or any vice that one cannot control. True religion, true Christianity, is bringing everything we are under the lordship of Jesus. It is giving more and more of ourselves to him and worshipping him. Let me be very clear: I am not saying that persons who become tamers of the tongue are perfect. Later, James said that nobody can tame the tongue (Jas 3:8). He used the tongue as an example of any sin that dominates us. We need to get those things that control us under control. Even if we are the greatest religious people in the world, our tongues or any controlling sins in our lives can give us away as being fake.

The tongue was obviously the issue for these people. It was the specific thing that they needed to deal with in their lives, for James spoke about the use of the tongue throughout this book. He warned people against justifying their sins with their speech and blaming God for their sins (Jas 1:13–14). He told them that they needed to be slow to speak and quick to listen and that they should listen more than they talk (Jas 1:19). He warned them specifically about using their tongues to show favoritism towards those with money and to make those who are poor feel bad about their poverty (Jas 2:3–4). He warned them against saying that they want to help people in need when they are unwilling to do anything to alleviate their problems (Jas 2:16). He warned them that the tongue is the strongest, fiercest member of the entire body, that it cannot ever be tamed, and that it can do great damage (Jas 3:1–12). He ended that section by reminding them that it is with the same mouth that they bless and curse the Lord. He condemned those who speak harshly against their brothers and judge them. He said that they are not doers of the law, but judges of it (Jas 4:11). He warned against boastful speaking about the future when they have no control over the future (Jas 4:13). Instead, they should be submitting themselves under the authority and sovereignty of the one who does know the future and saying, "if the Lord wills." I think James was specifically concerned about the tongue, don't you? He understood that it is one thing to say that we love God and love others and it is another thing actually to do it with our tongues under control.

Recently, I had the opportunity to apply this specific issue. There is something about sports that God uses to show us our character. There is something about our kids in sports that God really uses to show us our character. I am the catch-all coach for my kids' sports. One day at my youngest son's kindergarten soccer game, the ball was rolling across the face of the goal. He could have easily scored if he had used his right foot; but he had to stop, turn around, and kick it with his left foot. I yelled at him to use his other foot. I soon realized that maybe I was being too negative and quickly followed up that yell with a "but you're doing a great job." There were some other parents sitting by whose sons are in my son's class at school. They started to laugh at my quick change of tune. Later in the day, I found myself at my older son's third- and fourth-grade game. They were out of position, they were not playing hard, and they were standing around watching the ball. I was so frustrated I was yelling (politely, of course) at them to get back in their positions. I was thinking, "I am going to lose my sanctification." Then it hit me that what

I should be thinking is, "Your religion is worthless if you cannot control your tongue right now."

Think of it in these terms: What does the sermon have to do with that which controls me? Maybe it is the tongue, but maybe it is something else. Sermons in general are meant for us to deal with our sin and give more and more of our lives to Jesus, to submit more and more to him in every area. Specifically, the tongue may not always be mentioned; but lust, worldliness, or anger may be. What specifically are our self-control issues? Is the tongue standing before us as an example of something to show us that our religion has been worthless?

Second, how does this truth help me show compassion to the helpless? James continued, after dealing with the tongue, with the issue of compassion. How has the sermon made a difference in how I am showing love to others? James 1:27 is not meant to be a complete list of what it means to have pure, undefiled Christianity. These are mere expressions of what we should be doing as a result of the impact of the word of God upon us. Is the truth making a difference?

True religion is expressed in taking care of people. For James, that was orphans and widows. They were generally thought of as being unable to take care of themselves. According to James, real religion is developing a heart like that of the Lord himself. The psalmist wrote of the Lord, "The LORD protects the strangers; He supports the fatherless and the widow, but He thwarts the way of the wicked" (Ps 146:9; see Ps 68:5). Of course, we have the illustration of Jesus, who continually performed miracles not only to authenticate the message he was preaching but also to show compassion on people who were hurting.

We are about the gospel. We are about the truth. But if we are not about helping people who are struggling and having a hard time taking care of themselves, I think James would tell us that we are neither truly about the gospel nor about the truth.

Maybe the clearest example from Jesus concerning this compassion principle is found in his account of the Good Samaritan. Jesus' account targets the heart of biblical Christianity as to whether it is a theoretical or actual religion. Does it make a difference just in our minds or actually in the way we live in front of others? Jesus taught that a real love for God compels a person to love any person in need compassionately. The right teaching and thinking about Jesus and his word should produce the most compassionate people. Unfortunately, often this is not true. Sometimes Christians are dichotomized as either humanitarians or trutharians (people who only love truth). What Jesus said is that real truth should drive us to be humanitarians.

Many people read the account of the Good Samaritan as a good story about taking care of their neighbors. Once again, they fail to read it in context. Why did Jesus tell the story? He was in the middle of a conversation with his disciples when a lawyer stood up to ask him a question to test him: "What shall I do to inherit eternal life?" (Luke 10:25). This exact same question is asked by many people in our world today. Real Christianity answers this question. Although it was a good question, the emphasis of the question was wrong. The lawyer was concerned about what he had to do. The religious leaders of their day believed that eternal life with God was a reward for something they were able to accomplish on this earth. I am intrigued that Jesus did not seem to set him straight but responded by asking the man his thoughts on the question by asking him, "What is written in the Law? How does it read to you?" (Luke 10:26). In other words, Jesus asked this expert in the law what he thought the texts of Scripture had to say in regards to his question. Interestingly enough, Jesus was asking the man to look at the one common theme these two had, the authority of the Scriptures. Jesus wanted him to answer based upon the texts of the Old Testament, not based on oral tradition.

The lawyer gave a good summary of the entire law in the two basic laws of love: Love God with all that you are and love your neighbor as yourself. It was accurate for him to divide even the Ten Commandments into these classifications because the first four commandments deal with loving God and the last six deal with loving the neighbor. Jesus later acknowledged these as the two greatest commandments. Although the lawyer was able to articulate truth correctly, he had never internalized or lived that truth. It was only an answer to him. Darrell Bock said, "Devotion to God is expressed by devotion to others, so that there is no distinction between devotion to God and treatment of people. They go together. Jesus encourages total love for God and humankind."[8]

Jesus responded by saying, "You have answered correctly, do this and you will live" (Luke 10:28). He told him to go and do it. He acknowledged that it is one thing to know it but quite another thing to live it. It is one thing to be taught something or to hear something but quite

---

8. Bock, *Luke*, 1025.

another thing to live that truth. It is important to note that Jesus was not saying do these things and inherit eternal life, as if it is some calling of good works. Jesus was saying that a person will do these things if they have eternal life. This love is responsive, not causal. Loving God with all ours hearts and loving our neighbors as ourselves are not the cause of salvation but the response to it.

The lawyer did not like this answer and wanted to find some loopholes in the laws. That is why he asked the question in verse 29, "Who is my neighbor?" He wished to justify himself. He was trying to limit the demands of the law and thus his responsibilities. He was looking for the minimum obedience required. He was trying to do what many professing Christians have mastered: doing the least amount possible to be considered Christian. It is only based upon this interaction with the lawyer that the story of the Good Samaritan makes real sense:

> Jesus replied and said, "A man was going down from Jerusalem to Jericho, and fell among robbers, and they stripped him and beat him, and went away leaving him half dead. And by chance a priest was going down on that road, and when he saw him, he passed by on the other side. Likewise a Levite also, when he came to the place and saw him, passed by on the other side. But a Samaritan, who was on a journey, came upon him; and when he saw him, he felt compassion, and came to him and bandaged up his wounds, pouring oil and wine on them; and he put him on his own beast, and brought him to an inn and took care of him. On the next day he took out two denarii and gave them to the innkeeper and said, 'Take care of him; and whatever more you spend, when I return I will repay you.'" (Luke 10:30–35)

On the surface, this story is very easy to understand. A man on a journey from Jerusalem to Jericho was attacked by robbers. He was stripped of his clothes, beaten, and left half dead. This man was fighting for his life; he was in a miserable, desperate condition. It is assumed that this man was Jewish; for Christ was addressing a Jewish audience, and nearly everyone who made the journey on this well-known road was Jewish. People were identified in those days largely based on their clothes or their speech (or dialect). After the attack, this man was not identifiable by clothes or speech; he was anonymous to those who passed his way. As people came to him, they were not looking at him as Jew or Gentile or Samaritan. The man was any person, void of ethnic background, void of stature, void of position. Jesus wanted to drive home the point that he was a human being, a neighbor in need of help.

The robbers did not treat this man as their neighbor, which is obvious. They robbed him, stripped him, beat him, and left him for dead. But the priest was just as guilty as the robbers. Most people would think that if anyone was going to help, it would be a priest; but he crossed to the other side and ignored the man. Then a Levite who happened upon this man also passed by on the other side. Jesus was trying to make the same point to this lawyer that James made: Religiosity means nothing. Official religious Jews with authority had been given two opportunities to help the man and had failed both times. The climax of the story was that the only man who helped was a Samaritan.

As most people know, the Samaritans were despised by the Jews. They were the least respected people in the world. They were a mixed race of people, half-breeds created from the Jews and Gentile people who inhabited the land in which the Jews lived during the time of captivity. Righteous Jews could not stand them at all and avoided them. Yet it was a man from this despised people who was the hero of the story. When he came upon the man, he had compassion on him and helped him at great personal expense to himself. He did not care about himself or about religion but about taking care of this helpless man.

After telling the story, Jesus turned to the lawyer and asked one more question: "Which of these three do you think proved to be a neighbor to the man who fell into the robbers' hands?" (Luke 10:36). At the beginning, the lawyer was trying to ask specifically who his neighbor was; but Jesus turned it around on him and asked who proved to be a neighbor. The proper question is not about who our neighbors are, as if there is some localized, limited group of people we are to love. The proper question is about us living as good neighbors. The intention of compassionate, real Christianity is not about to whom we minister but about our ministering to everyone in need: "Neighborliness is not found in a racial bond, nationality, color, gender, proximity, or by living in a certain neighborhood. We become a neighbor by responding sensitively to the needs of others . . . The issue is not who we may or may not serve, but serving where need exists. We are not to seek to limit who our neighbors might be. Rather, we are to be a neighbor to those whose needs we can meet."[9]

9. Ibid., 1035.

Live the Preaching of God's Word   121

The point is that all truth should be shaping and changing us into more compassionate people. As we sit under the preaching of God's word and then walk out, we need to be asking ourselves how this is changing us more into the image of Jesus Christ, who showed compassion on everyone he met. How are we moved to help those who need help?

Third, how does this truth help me keep myself unstained by the world? James added at the end of chapter 1 a portion of Scripture that some see as no more than a little tag: Pure and undefiled religion is "to keep oneself unstained by the world" (Jas 1:27). Responding to the word of God should be a purifying tool in our lives. When we respond to the preaching of God's word, when we force ourselves joyfully to live the word preached, we are in essence saying that the things of God mean more to us than the things of the world: "Living in the world but not 'of the world,' the believer must be alert to the danger of having the contamination of the world 'rub off' on him."[10] The Apostle John defined the things of the world as the lust of the flesh, the lust of the eyes, and the boastful pride of life (1 John 2:16). We should always be seeking to rid ourselves of these things throughout the week. We come to church to hear a word from the Lord through the preaching of his word so that we may remain unstained by the world.

Jesus clearly gave his opinion to this matter when he prayed for his disciples right before he was betrayed and went to the cross. While in the garden, Jesus prayed,

> I am no longer in the world; and yet they themselves are in the world, and I come to You. Holy Father, keep them in Your name, the name which You have given Me, that they may be one even as We are. While I was with them, I was keeping them in Your name which You have given Me; and I guarded them and not one of them perished but the son of perdition, so that the Scripture would be fulfilled. But now I come to You; and these things I speak in the world so that they may have My joy made full in themselves. I have given them Your word; and the world has hated them, because they are not of the world, even as I am not of the world. I do not ask You to take them out of the world, but to keep them from the evil one. They are not of the world, even as I am not of the world. Sanctify them in the truth; Your word is truth. As You sent Me into the world, I also have sent them into

---

10. Hiebert, *James*, 127.

the world. For their sakes I sanctify Myself, that they themselves also may be sanctified in truth. (John 17:11–19).

Jesus is concerned with our interactions with the world. As he prayed, he focused on the fact that he had been keeping them in the Father's name (except for Judas). But Jesus knew that he was no longer going to be with them to protect them. There were a few options at this point. Jesus could just take them with him when he left this earth. But that had not been the plan from the beginning. Jesus confessed that he had given them the word of God and that the world hated them. Jesus asked the Father not to take them out of the world but that he protect them from the evil one (v. 15). Christ was praying for protection. He was concerned that the evil one would tempt them and that they would give in to sin.

But it was not just a prayer for protection. It was positively a prayer for sanctification. How were they to be sanctified? How are we to be sanctified? Through the truth of his word. We are sanctified and thereby protected from the world when the truth of God makes an impact upon our lives. When we are listening to the truth of God through the preaching of his word, we should be asking ourselves what specifically does this have to say about our holiness. How can this help keep us unstained by the world?

We often take for granted the people who will respond to us in emergencies. We live in a place where emergency first-response teams are numerous and available. We have emergency medical services (EMS), fire departments, and police officers. What if someone had a major accident or some tragedy at home, called 911, and received this response: "Okay, thank you for calling. We will get someone there as soon as we can, but they are in the middle of the football game, so let them finish first and then they will be ready to respond to you." The person with the emergency might respond by saying, "No, your job is to respond when you are called." Is it fair to say, Christians, that our job is to respond to the Scriptures when we are called? After each sermon, we should specifically ask how does this sermon helps us (1) control that which controls us, (2) show compassion to the helpless, and (3) keep ourselves unstained by the world? Friends, let us all respond with specifics.

RESPOND WITH DEPENDENCE

One church I attended in college used to put at the bottom of the sermon notes page in the bulletin this statement: "It is your responsibility to make sure to apply the truth of this sermon to your life." That's a good statement, yet it leaves me empty. We do need to take responsibility for the application of the truth in our lives. However, this statement not only releases preachers of any sort of responsibility in helping people apply the truth to their lives but also fails to acknowledge proper reliance upon the Lord in applying the truth to our lives.

Remember Jesus' conclusion to the Sermon on the Mount? What does it mean that the wise man built his house upon the rock? The concept of this building is a metaphor for living one's life. It means every ambition, thought, word, and deed is a call to live under the lordship of Jesus.

But what is the rock? The famous children's song says the rock is building one's life on the Lord Jesus Christ. It is true that we should build our lives upon the Lord, but that is not the point of the illustration of the rock used by Jesus. The rock is a reference to living a life that responds to the words of Jesus. It is living a life that obeys the truth it hears from the Bible. Hearing the words of Jesus and acting on them are equivalent to building the house upon the rock. It is what James said about being doers of the word and not just hearers only.

The point is that the proper response to the words of Jesus is the life that obeys his words and trusts him to take care of what happens. It is not a response in our self-righteousness. It is not trusting our own efforts but trusting him in all things. It is only in that sense that we build our lives on the Lord.

In contrast to the wise man is the foolish man who does not dig at all. He is not trusting in the Lord. He may claim to be a follower of Jesus, but there is no dependence on Jesus in him. He is the man who walks out of the church service saying, "I can do this myself. I don't need anyone to help me, especially some guy who lived a couple of thousand years ago. I can work at my own religion." That is foolishness.

Let me take this one step further. Throughout the listening process described in this book, there has been a plea for us to depend upon the Holy Spirit to help us listen. I said at the beginning that we need to pray before the sermon in anticipation of the sermon, for it shows that we are dependent for him to work in our hearts. Then in the discernment process, I encouraged us all to listen prayerfully and spiritually. As we are listening to truth in the hope of discerning whether it is true or false, there should be a prayer in our hearts that we need the help of the Holy Spirit in the process. Well, guess what? We need to pray and beg for the help of the Holy Spirit in this step of living the preached word of God as well. We will never be great at living the truth of sermons if we are not leaving sermons with reliance upon the Holy Spirit in our lives. We must be dependent upon him to help us walk differently based upon the truth that he has taught us. Friends, let us respond with dependence.

RESPOND WITH COMPLETENESS

I am intrigued by the end of the Sermon on the Mount, not just the message Jesus spoke but the response of the people. After Jesus finished speaking, "the crowds were amazed at His teaching; for He was teaching them as one having authority, and not as their scribes" (Matt 7:28–29). The people left that sermon amazed at his teaching. The wording indicates the idea of being dumfounded or astonished. Literally, it reads "struck out of their senses."[11] These people walked away from the greatest sermon ever preached thinking about what Jesus had said and what it meant. The words of Jesus were different from anything they had heard before; powerful, so convicting, and influential. Of course, the God of truth manifested before them was going to be fairly good at teaching. But what was it that held them in awe?

They were in awe because Jesus spoke in ways that their scribes had never spoken. The scribes taught out of their traditions; Jesus taught out of the truth of God. Jesus did not just deal with external issues; he dealt with their hearts. He talked about the real things of hatred, lust, worry, and other practical issues; the scribes and Pharisees talked about tithing their spices (Matt 23:23). Jesus really cared for the people; the other teachers of the day were more concerned about religion than people. The people were in awe because Jesus taught with authority.

I have this image of Jesus in my mind that after he prayed at the close of the sermon, he went down to the bottom of the hill and greeted everyone as they left. (I know it did not happen, but play the scenario with me.) On their way out, they were continually telling him that he was the best preacher that they had heard. They said that he was much

---

11. Hendriksen, *Matthew*, 382.

better than the other preachers in town. They told him that they would be back next Sunday. They told him that they loved it on the Sundays he preached. They loved him as a communicator and as a preacher. He was their absolute favorite preacher.

But (ready for this?) nowhere in Scripture does it say anything about them acting on the sermon they had just heard. They were just warned that they needed to respond to the sermon. We are not told of anything they did.

We need to remember that it is one thing to be in awe of Jesus—his person, his works, his words—and quite another thing to be obedient to him. To put it another way, it is one thing to be in awe of a sermon, a text of Scripture, a message, or a preacher and quite another thing to act on it. We do not know what happened exactly to those people at the Sermon on the Mount; but not long after this, we are told of some men who came to him struggling with his call to discipleship (Matt 8:18–34). Boice says, "The text does not say that any who heard him then believed in his doctrine or committed themselves to him. I am sure some did. Some do today. But sadly, in our hectic, more sophisticated century, it is even more possible to do what the majority must have done in that day: let the hour of salvation pass by."[12]

How many times have we ever walked out of a sermon or small group Bible study or adult Sunday school class saying it was a wonderful sermon, it was a wonderful lesson, it was totally enthralling; yet nothing changed. Soon we forget even what the preacher talked about. That is what the foolish builder did. That is what the forgetful hearer does: hears it, maybe even says it was awesome, and then leaves and does nothing about it. This is why I say we need to respond with completeness.

Do not be half-hearted. Good intentions will not do at this point. Hell is filled with people with good intentions. It does not mean that we pick and choose what to obey from the sermon, but that we are quick to obey and follow all that we possibly can. Can we imagine the person who struggles with anger hearing this sermon that Jesus preached? He hears Jesus preach on lust and says, "I can do that." He hears preaching on worry and says, "I can do that." But the one that he needs to do is to listen to the instruction on anger and murder. That is responding with completeness: dealing with what we need to deal with. Friends, let us respond with completeness.

12. Boice, *Gospel of Matthew*, 117.

What are you known for? Larry Walters will always be known for one thing. A thirty-three-year-old man from Long Beach, California, Larry decided he wanted to see his neighborhood from a new perspective. He went to the local army surplus store one morning and bought forty-five used weather balloons. That afternoon, he strapped himself into a lawn chair to which several of his friends tied the now helium-filled balloons. He took a six-pack of beer, a peanut butter and jelly sandwich, a parachute, a CB radio, and a BB gun, figuring he could shoot the balloons one at a time when he was ready to land. Walters, who assumed the balloons would lift him about one hundred feet in the air, was caught off guard when the chair soared more than 16,000 feet into the sky; right in the middle of the air traffic pattern of Los Angeles International Airport. Too frightened to shoot any of the balloons, he stayed airborne for more than two hours, forcing the airport to shut down its runways for much of the afternoon and causing long delays in flights across the country. Finally, he shot some of the balloons and started his trip back to earth. Almost down, the ropes to the balloons became entangled in power lines, causing a twenty-minute blackout in the Long Beach area. Soon after he was safely grounded and cited by the police, reporters asked him three questions: Were you scared? To which he responded yes. Would you do it again? To which he responded no. Why did you do it? To which he responded, "Because you can't just sit there!"

Real Christianity does not just sit there. We are not here just to be sermon junkies, hoping to be filled with the next text of Scripture and that's it. Real Christianity makes waves because of the application of the Bible to our lives. We are to receive the preaching of God's word, examine it, accept it, and then live it. We are to put it into action so that people look at our lives and say that we are living sermons.

That does not mean it is easy. There are many things that make living the sermon difficult. The last chapter will deal with some of the hindrances of preaching that make listening and living preaching tough. Regardless, we are to persevere in the preaching and listening of God's word.

5

Persevere the Preaching of God's Word

LIFE IS FILLED WITH inspirational stories of people who have overcome amazing odds to achieve amazing results. Take for instance, Lance Armstrong. At the young age of twenty-five, this young, promising bicyclist was diagnosed with testicular cancer. The cancer had spread quickly, being found throughout his abdomen, lungs, and lymph nodes. After aggressive treatment, Armstrong was at first given a 75 percent chance of survival, which soon dropped to 40 percent when the doctors found cancer in his brain. The rest of the story is one of epic proportions, only the kind of results normally found in the movies.

Two years later, in 1999, he won the Tour de France for the first time and continued to win it for seven straight years until his retirement in 2005. From 2002 to 2005, Armstrong was named the Associated Press Male Athlete of the Year. He has said that although he is a seven-time winner of the Tour de France, he is mostly a full-time cancer survivor.[1] He has overcome amazing odds to achieve amazing results.

The same story can be said of countless people in our world who face amazing challenges and overcome them to achieve amazing results. Probably some of the best stories are those the world has never heard. They are of our friends, aunts, cousins, grandfathers, and so on.

The purpose of this chapter is to help us think through the things that we all need to overcome when it comes to listening to the preaching of God's word. There are many obstacles that we all face each week when the preacher stands up to preach the Bible. Although we have already dealt with many of them previously, I want to fill in the gaps with some of the issues not yet dealt with that prevent us from listening effectively to the preaching of God's word.

---

1. Armstrong, "Personal Information," line 1.

OVERCOMING SHALLOW VIEWS OF PREACHING

Many people do not appreciate preaching. Odds are that if you're picking up this book, you have some appreciation for the act of preaching. But I also acknowledge that there may be some who skipped chapter 1 to get to the really practical aspects of listening. For those people, this section may not make any sense.

The Apostle Paul said that in his preaching, he was "a fragrance of Christ to God among those who are being saved and among those who are perishing; to the one an aroma from death to death, to the other an aroma from life to life" (2 Cor 2:15–16). Biblical preaching always draws a line in the sand. As Paul preached God's word, some people were coming to life. Others were being confirmed to death. But many people want to redefine or water down what preaching should be.

In its simplest form, preaching is explaining of the text and applying it to the hearer. Preaching is what Lloyd-Jones said is "a transaction between the preacher and the listener."[2] Unfortunately, what has happened is that people take a definition like that and divorce it from the text of the Scripture. Therefore, preaching has subtly become only an interaction between a preacher and a listener apart from the Scriptures. It has subtly become less and less about the text of Scripture. As a result, it should be called preaching less and less. Biblical expositor Steve Lawson said,

> A new way of "doing" church is emerging. In this radical paradigm shift, exposition is being replaced with entertainment, preaching with performances, doctrine with drama, and theology with theatrics. The pulpit, once the focal point of the church, is now being overshadowed by the variety of church—growth techniques, everything from trendy worship styles to glitzy presentations and vaudeville-like pageantries. In seeking to capture the upper hand in church growth, a new wave of pastors is reinventing church and repackaging the gospel into a product to be sold to "consumers."[3]

In recent days, preaching has morphed even into emergent conversations. In many places, preaching is either downplayed so significantly that it has little impact or completely ignored and dismissed as irrelevant. Some people may say and think things similar to these: "Preaching does not work anymore. We need to make it more entertaining. We need

---

2. Lloyd-Jones, *Preaching & Preachers*, 53.
3. Lawson, *Famine in the Land*, 25.

to give away free cappuccino each week. We need to do all these other things to soften the force of preaching. If it's still too confrontational, simply get rid of preaching altogether and have conversations with each other to discover what God might be trying to say to us." It is these thoughts that we must overcome if we are going to be effective listeners to preaching. We must be very leery of the attitude of the people described in 2 Timothy 4:3 who "will not endure sound doctrine" and want "to have their ears tickled, [so] they will accumulate for themselves teachers in accordance to their own desires."

How do we overcome shallow views of preaching? *First, support our preachers.* It was noted in chapter 3 that it is very beneficial to build relationships with our preachers to the best of our ability as the size of our churches allow. The author of the book of Hebrews gave this advice to all of us in the church: "Obey your leaders and submit to them, for they keep watch over your souls as those who will give an account. Let them do this with joy and not with grief, for this would be unprofitable for you" (Heb 13:17). It is to our benefit to support and submit to our preachers so that they have joy in leading us. We must trust the Scriptures when they say that it is more profitable for us if we do this as opposed to not doing it.

There are many ways we can support our preachers (many of them have already been stated throughout this book). We can send them thank you notes about what we are learning from their preaching. We can schedule times when we can share with them personally in their offices or at lunch how much we have grown from their preaching. We can schedule some time with them just to meet with them and pray for them concerning their upcoming schedules. We can uplift them in prayer every day by praying for their study and concentration. We can all think of other ways we can support our preachers, yet the greatest way is to apply the sermons that they preach to our lives.

Second, support our churches financially. Jesus said that our hearts will go where our money goes: "Where your treasure is, there your heart will be also" (Matt 6:21). If we want to overcome shallow views of preaching, then we must support biblical preaching with our wallets. We should desire to free our preachers so that they can live average lifestyles and not be distracted from preaching because of taking care of their families. This may not sound like that big of a deal to many, but my experience is that the first thing to go when people are not happy with their preachers is their money. When preachers do something or say something offensive to some people, those people are tempted to withdraw their support from the ministry. I am not saying that we should remain under men in the pulpit who have character that would disqualify them from the ministry. What I am saying is that people with shallow views of preaching are the ones who give only when the messages are good for them.

Paul's point in saying that "each one must do just as he has purposed in his heart, not grudgingly or under compulsion, for God loves a cheerful giver" (2 Cor. 9:7) is not that we should withhold our money if we are feeling under compulsion. Rather, he meant that we need to make radical attitude adjustments so that we give with joy out of generosity of all that God has given us. If we give joyfully to the ministry of preaching at our local churches, then we will have vested interest in what takes place there. If that happens, we are more likely to support the preaching of God's word in other ways. In dealing with our hearts in giving, Randy Alcorn said, "Do you wish you cared more about eternal things? Then reallocate some of your money, maybe *most* of your money, from temporal things to eternal things. Watch what happens. God wants your heart. He isn't looking just for "donors" for His kingdom, those who stand outside the cause and dispassionately consider acts of philanthropy. He's looking for disciples immersed in the causes they give to. He wants people so filled with a vision for eternity that they wouldn't dream of not investing their money, time, and prayers where they will matter most."[4]

Third, invite the preaching of difficult subjects. There are some topics about which preachers have a difficult time preaching. One such topic is what we've just discussed: giving and money. Many preachers feel it may come across as self-serving. Another difficult topic is submission to church leaders. I am sure anyone can guess the reason that is a difficult topic for preachers to preach. There are also some doctrinal issues, such as the doctrine of election and same-sex marriage. There are social issues, such as poverty. Still, if we want to overcome shallow views of preaching, then we should ask our preachers to preach on subjects that are normally difficult for us to hear. This is just the opposite of those people that Paul said would someday only surround themselves by preachers who tickled their ears (2 Tim 4:3–4). Unless we think this is not an issue, consider

---

4. Alcorn, *Treasure Principle*, 44–45.

this: I have a friend who is told the topics he is not allowed to address in the pulpit each week. He is living what Paul told Timothy.

Recently, I was asked if our church would be interested in conducting a worship service at the Kansas State Fair. With joy, I took about one hundred people with me to minister to the other couple of hundred people there. As I was praying about what to preach, the Lord laid on my heart the second coming of Jesus from Revelation 19:11–16. If you have not read that recently, you may be shocked to know that it is a gruesome picture of judgment and torment that will happen when Jesus finally comes back to this earth. For about thirty minutes, I preached the gruesomeness of this text with the big idea that understanding Jesus as the Warrior Messiah will help people understand mercy and grace. When Jesus comes back, he is coming to judge; but for now, he is offering mercy and grace so that when he does come back we can be on his team, not in opposition to him. This was not an easy message to preach.

Afterwards, I had many people not from our church telling me that I had guts to preach on something so judgmental. I preached it because I felt the Lord leading me, and I knew I had the support of those from my church to preach on any subject. They trust me. They want the word of God preached, which means that they are fighting against ear tickling. That is freeing for a preacher.

If we want to overcome shallow views of preaching, we should be willing to invite our preachers to preach on controversial subjects. Then when they do, we should thank them and tell them how much we needed it.

Fourth, endure any persecution that may arise from the preaching of God's word. If our churches take strong stances on the gospel, Scriptures, and preaching, there will be persecution. It may come in subtle forms, such as looks and stereotypes from people when they find out that we go to one of "those" churches. It may come in blatant forms, such as picketing, or even in extreme forms of violence. I say this because literally every time in the Scriptures that preaching happened, there were those who responded positively and those who hated what was being said. For every person that loves preaching, there are hundreds who despise biblical preaching. Unfortunately, many of them are even in the church. People who want to hear from God will learn to love preaching even in a world that is growing more and more hateful of it.

We need to prepare ourselves, for if we believe in preaching and support preachers that preach the word, give our money to support those ministries, and even invite the preaching of difficult subjects, there will be persecution. When Paul went to the church of Thessalonica, we are told that the people imitated Paul, "having received the word in much tribulation with the joy of the Holy Spirit" (1 Thess 1:6). What does it mean that they suffered tribulations? We are given one example in the life of Jason, Paul's friend. He opened his home to give shelter to Paul and his associates. Because of the preaching of God's word and the message that was preached, there was a group of people who came to his house and dragged him off before the civil authorities (Acts 17:5–9). They accused him of partaking in this great crime simply because he housed Paul and his associates.

The persecution did not stop with Jason in Thessalonica. According to Luke, "But when the Jews of Thessalonica found out that the word of God had been proclaimed by Paul in Berea also, they came there as well, agitating and stirring up the crowds" (Acts 17:13). I am not sure we can imagine a situation in which persecution is so bad that the preacher has to leave and go to another city and people from the first city follow him there to persecute him. Although it may be hard for American Christians to understand, it does happen overseas in places with less religious freedom. Yet I wonder if the day is coming that it will happen here as well. We need to prepare ourselves for a time when overcoming these shallow views of preaching will be harder. I assume that in ten or twenty years, this will be an even greater issue than it is now. Friends, let us overcome shallow views of preaching.

OVERCOMING OUR LEARNING STYLE

It does not take long in any sort of educational setting to realize that people learn differently. Do we know how we perceive or process information most effectively? How we learn? When it comes to learning styles, it is generally accepted that there are three general categories: auditory learners, visual learners, and tactile-kinesthetic learners. What I mean by overcoming learning styles is that we should not use our learning styles as an excuse for not listening to the preaching of God's word. We cannot simply say that because we are visual learners and the preacher presents in an auditory way, we cannot learn or listen. That just will not do. Like any good athlete, we need to push through our hindrances and work hard at our listening. How do we do it? Let me explain each of the learning styles and give some advice about learning from the preacher through our learning styles instead of using them as crutches.

Auditory learners are people who learn best when information is presented orally. They are very analytical and cognitive in nature. From a teacher's standpoint, the most obvious strategies allowing auditory learners to thrive include "lecture, discussion, independent work, objective presentation and practice, questioning techniques or tasks that require exact or specific answers, activities that involve memory, and verbal sorting."[5] These are great for those who sit under the preaching of God's word, for preaching is mostly oral in nature. I have wondered if churches are primarily filled with people who are auditory learners because they are drawn to the preaching of God's word. There is very little that these people need to do to overcome their learning style. Strong auditory learners will not even desire to take notes because that is a distraction. They want simply to sit there, retain, and learn.

Recently I had a conversation with someone who is a self-described auditory learner. He said that when PowerPoint is used in the sermon, it is distracting. If you are auditory and are negatively affected by visuals that are given during the service, try not to look at them. Focus only on the preacher and nothing else.

The one danger for auditory learners is comprehension. It will be helpful after the sermon is over to have review sessions with someone. This will drive the point home even more for them. For them, gathering in the foyer after the sermon should be to review what was preached.

Visual learners are people who learn from visual aids and mental images. These are people who have to see it before they can completely understand it. They really connect through the illustrations and word pictures in sermons. This is very difficult because sermons are not generally visual in nature. Certainly, this is why many in the church today want to use videos and other creative arts to help visual learners. Yet, if preachers do not do any of these things, there are still several things visual learners can do to overcome their learning style. *First, take notes.* Seeing the outline on paper as they write it down will help these persons engage with their preachers even more. This technique is especially helpful in reviewing sermons as they think about what their preachers

---

5. Sarasin, *Learning Style Perspectives,* 45–46.

said. They can look back at the outlines and thus learn visually through their own words.

Second, ask the preacher to use PowerPoint, at least for his main points, if at all possible. In contrast to my one friend who is auditory and is distracted by PowerPoint, another friend recently told me that seeing a simple outline on a screen in front of him helps him follow the preacher better. It helps him reengage when his mind wanders. It helps him trace the flow of the text of Scripture.

Third, affirm the use of illustrations and word pictures in the preacher's sermons. Visual learners especially learn through illustrations and word pictures that preachers use. It may not be the wisest use of our time to ask our preachers to use more illustrations, but we can affirm their use of vivid word pictures or helpful illustrations when they occur. Be specific. (Preachers are often slow learners.) After the service, make a special note to inform the preacher of how helpful the use of the word pictures and illustrations was in the process of sharing the truth through the sermon. Whatever we do as visual learners, we must not use our learning style as a crutch. The message of God can be heard even if it takes more work to do so.

Tactile-kinesthetic learners will have the most work in overcoming their learning styles to get the most out of sermons. These are people who learn best when they are doing something or are involved in the process. Vivid illustrations, word pictures, and outlines may help to some extent to the tactile-kinesthetic learner as they will help these persons engage and be part of the learning experience. When they take notes, it is as if the message is going in and then out of them, helping them to process the information. Yet, these will not do enough to help them learn.

One thing this type of learner can do is to hold the Scriptures in their hands as the preacher reads them. Another thing that tactile-kinesthetic learners can do is to study ahead. Most preachers plan their preaching, so tactile-kinesthetic learners can ask their preachers the texts they will be preaching the next week. Then, these learners should spend some time in those texts before the sermon. As they read them, they may find it helpful to read while they stand or as they walk. They could write out the text for the sermon on note cards and have them with them for the sermon.

These are simple suggestions that may or may not help each individual. Each person should seek to know themselves as to how they learn best. Each person will have a time when they are engaged with the preacher. When that happens, take the time to evaluate what was different in that situation. Once that has been evaluated, they should seek to mimic those things they had done. The most important part of this process is to engage preachers and be part of the preaching process. I suggested these ideas to someone just a few weeks ago when we were talking about how boring church was for him. He was not getting anything out of the sermons. He explained that as the preacher moved on to verse five, he was still in verse two, distracted by something it said. I challenged him to read and study the text on Saturday night before the sermon to see if that kept him engaged on Sunday morning. After church on Sunday, he told me that doing so had really helped him follow the preaching of God's word that day.

Whether we are auditory, visual, or tactile-kinesthetic, our learning styles cannot be an excuse for us not hearing from God's word. I cannot imagine people of Israel saying to a prophet condemning them for not listening to the word of the Lord that they would have listened if the presentation had been visual, that because the sermon was auditory they simply could not learn from it. That is foolishness. We have a responsibility. Each person has been uniquely created for a certain purpose, and the One who created us wants us to hear his message from his word as it is preached.

The one thing that we must not forget to do is to pray. Plead with the One who created learning styles to help us engage our preachers and learn from them in spite of our learning orientations. Friends, let us all overcome our learning styles.

OVERCOMING THE INTERNET PREACHER

We live in an age of accessibility to preachers and sermons unlike any other time in the history of the church. For those who live in cities without good, Bible-teaching churches, there are solutions. I call them Internet preachers; but in days past, they were radio and TV preachers. With the invention of the Internet and podcasts, there are more sermons going out to the world each week than one can imagine. Most churches that used to charge for sermons are now giving them away.

As I write this, of the top twenty podcasts under the banner of religion and spirituality on ITunes, there are at least five that I consider good biblical preachers.[6] There are also some centralized Web sites to which almost any preacher can upload sermons to be downloaded. One such site is www.sermonaudio.com, which claims that for Sunday, September 27, 2009, they had 595,525 page views with 55,452 downloads. They claimed over two million sermons were downloaded in the past thirty-one days. That is an astronomical number of sermons being downloaded from the Internet. Mark Driscoll has claimed to have well over one million sermons downloaded each year from his Web site, www.marshillchurch.org. John MacArthur has literally thousands of sermons to which one can listen or download free from his Web site, www.gty.org, as does John Piper on www.desiringgod.org. I could keep listing resource after resource for good, free sermons to which one can listen and find nourishment.

Many of these Internet preachers are also involved in multisite churches, with their sermons being fed through video to screens at different locations. In the May/June *9Marks eJournal*, Matt Chandler, who is part of a multisite church, gave this solemn warning on the dangers of multisite churches: "The problem that haunts us is a simple one. Where does this idea lead? Where does this end? Twenty years from now are there fifteen preachers in the United States?"[7] The danger of multisite churches is the same as that of Internet preachers: We may be tempted to get to the place where we only listen to the top fifteen preachers in the world.

Yes, we should feel blessed by the age of technology in which we live; and yes, it can be dangerous. With the good comes the danger that some people may listen to the preaching of some of the greatest preachers in the world today and then go to their churches on Sunday and be discouraged and disappointed in their own preachers each week. This can be devastating to any preacher!

I have felt that temptation from both sides of the equation. I have felt that temptation personally from the life of the listener. I love to listen to sermons. I love to hear what is going on around the world. I love to hear how different gifted men package the text of God's word to be heard and understood by their listeners. Over the years, I have found a few

---

6. Mark Driscoll of Mars Hill Church in Seattle is #3; John Piper of Bethlehem Baptist in Minneapolis is #6; Francis Chan of Cornerstone Church in Simi Valley, California is #9; Matt Chandler of the Village Church in Highland Village, Texas, is #13; Alistair Begg of Parkside Church in Cleveland is #18. Some other of the top 20 include Charles Stanley, Andy Stanley, and R. C. Sproul. These rankings are as of September 28, 2009.

7. Chandler, "Clouds on the Horizon," para. 4.

of my favorite preachers to whom I listen; and I have been tempted to think, "I wish my preacher was more like them."

I have also felt the comparison from the other side of the equation. Being a young preacher, as I listen to many preachers, I have been tempted to imitate their preaching styles instead of becoming the preacher that God wants me to be. I have been tempted to think, "If I was more like them, people would like my preaching better."

If we compare our preachers to those on the Internet, we are on a path headed to a place we do not want to go. Let me help with this, for there are several things that we can do to overcome this possible temptation. *First, remember the nature of spiritual gifts.* The Apostle Paul said, "Now there are varieties of gifts, but the same Spirit. And there are varieties of ministries, and the same Lord. There are varieties of effects, but the same God who works all things in all persons. But to each one is given the manifestation of the Spirit for the common good" (1 Cor 12:4–7). Later in his letter to the church at Ephesus, Paul wrote, "But to each one of us grace was given according to the measure of Christ's gift" (Eph 4:7). Paul also said, "We have gifts that differ according to the grace given to us" (Rom 12:6). John MacArthur said,

> Each believer's gift is unique. The measure or specific portion given is by sovereign design from the Head of the church. The Lord has measured out the exact proportion of each believer's gift . . . The exact proportion of enabling grace on the part of God is linked with the exact proportion of enacting faith on the part of each believer; and God is the source of both. The sum of this is that God gives both the grace and the faith to energize whatever gift He gives to the full intent of His purpose . . . We each have a gift that is measured out to us—with certain distinct capabilities, parameters, and purposes.[8]

All Christians have spiritual gifts but not all Christians with the same gift have the same measure of that gift. Maybe the clearest, most vivid example in the Scriptures comes in the parable of the talents (Matt 25:14–30). In the parable, a man entrusted his slaves with different talents (money) to be used. To one he gave five, to another two, and to another one. He left, saying that he would be back at some point. The one with five used them to gain another five so that he had ten in total; the one with two used his to double them as well; but the man with one

---

8. MacArthur, *Ephesians*, 135–36.

talent hid it in the ground, afraid of losing it. When the business owner returned, he was pleased with the five- and two-talent men but not with the one-talent man. The point of the parable is that we should all be very careful to use every opportunity the Lord has given us to the degree that he has given us.

The preachers ranked high on the ITunes podcast list are more than likely much more gifted than the preachers at our churches, and that is okay. In God's sovereignty, he decided to gift those men differently from most people with the same gift of teaching. That does not mean we cannot learn from them. We should. What it does mean, however, is that we should be careful not to compare them (five-talent gift people) with those with two-talent gifts.

Imagine we are given the gift of service equivalent to two talents. Do we want to be compared to the persons who serve next to us who have the gift of service equivalent to five talents? Of course not! The next time we are tempted to compare our preachers to someone on the national stage, remember that it is the Lord who has given the measure of gifts.

Second, remember the nature of the church. Jesus said in Matthew 16:18, "I will build My church." The church is his, not mine or yours or our preachers'. It is ultimately being built by Jesus himself. The problem is that not all places that call themselves churches are actually churches. In the town where I live, there are many places that call themselves churches but deny the Jesus of the Bible as the only hope of salvation. There are some who deny that the Bible is the full revelation of God. There are some that say that the words *hell* and *sin* are inappropriate ever to say (my thought is that if Jesus said it, it is okay to say.) These places are not what I am defining as churches.

When I say that we need to remember the nature of the church, I have in mind what Mark Driscoll said in a working definition of a church: "The local church is a community of regenerated believers who confess Jesus Christ as Lord. In obedience to Scripture they organize under qualified leadership, gather regularly for preaching and worship, observe the biblical sacraments of baptism and Communion, are unified by the Spirit, are disciplined for holiness, and scatter to fulfill the Great Commandment and the Great Commission as missionaries to the world for God's glory and their joy."[9]

9. Driscoll and Breshears, *Vintage Church*, 38.

If we really understand the church, we will realize that it is Jesus who places men in leadership within the church. He does this primarily through the people of a church affirming the call of a man to an office. Sometimes, people in the church mess it up and affirm calls to men who should not be in the pulpit. Regardless, we need ultimately to trust God in the giving of leaders to the church. He has gifted some people to shepherd his church under the chief shepherd, Jesus (1 Pet 5:1–4).

Although the Bible often talks about the universal church, the primary emphasis in the passages on gifts given to the church is in the context of a local assembly. How does this work itself out in the life of the local church? After Paul evangelized the island of Crete with his dear friend Titus, he left Titus there to organize the churches that had been planted. Paul knew that even in worship services, things were to be conducted properly in a decent, orderly manner (1 Cor 14:40). He also knew that the churches in every city needed organized leadership. In Titus 1:5, we see that Paul left Titus there to "set in order what remains and appoint elders in every city as I directed you." Paul then launched into a list of qualifications for the elders (pastors), culminating in the requirement that they are to be men who are "holding fast the faithful word" (v. 9).

This point cannot escape us as we are tempted to compare our preachers to any Internet preacher: Our preachers know us and our struggles much better than someone we have never met! This means that they are better suited to preach and help us apply the text of Scripture to our current situations. They know our families. They know our job situations. They know our struggles.

Some people may claim that their preachers do not really know them. Maybe they go to larger churches or do not have any relationship with their preachers. They may not think it should matter if they receive their primary nourishment from preachers on the Internet instead of the preachers in their churches However, in response to that, let me ask one very difficult question: Is there any chance that their preachers have not reached their potential as preachers? "Is it possible they are not the preachers they could be because they are too busy doing the work of the congregants and have very little time to work on their sermons? Maybe their preaching would be better and they would have more time to spend with the people in their church if the people in their church worked harder in the ministry." John Stott spoke against a false view of the preacher to hold onto all things in the ministry:

> If the pastor holds all the ecclesiastical reins in his own hands, and has no concept of a shared responsibility which involves lay leaders, then of course he has no time to study. But if he has grasped the New Testament image of the church as the Body of Christ, every member of which has been gifted for some form of ministry, then he will be continuously on the look-out for the gifts which God has given, in order to encourage people to recognize, develop, and exercize [sic] them . . . "Partnership" is the more biblical concept, so that clergy and laity rejoice in the variety of gifts which God has given, and help each other to use their gifts and fulfill their callings for the building up of Christ's Body.[10]

I want to be clear, there is an onus upon the leaders of churches to equip and let go of ministries. But do not miss this point: Sometimes they are not able to let go of ministries because we are not pulling our weight in the body of Christ. How foolish is it for us to compare Internet preachers with our preachers and put them over our preachers, who are trying to do their jobs and ours as well? Friends, let us overcome Internet preachers.

OVERCOMING THE TECHNOLOGY AGE

With all the things available today, technology can really be a detriment to our listening to preaching from God's word. Almost twenty-five years ago, Neil Postman wrote the classic book *Amusing Ourselves to Death*. In many ways, he was a futurist. The situation he described has been magnified in today's culture. He subtitled his book *Public Discourse in the Age of Show Business* because he wrote to show how television was undermining all other forms of communication. I am sure if he were alive today (he died at the age of 72 in 2003) even he might be shocked at the technology age.

His son, Andrew Postman, in a preface for the twentieth anniversary edition said, "Today's eighteen-to-twenty-two-year-olds live in a vastly different media environment from the one that existed in 1985. Their relationship to TV differs. Back then, MTV was in its late infancy. Today, news scrolls and corner-of-the-screen promos and "reality" shows and infomercials and nine hundred channels are the norm. And TV no longer dominates the media landscape. "Screen time" also means

---

10. Stott, *Between Two Worlds*, 205–6.

hours spent in front of the computer, video monitor, cell phone, and hand-held. Multitasking is standard. Communities have been replaced by demographics. Silence has been replaced by background noise. It's a different world."[11]

Although many things have changed, some things have continued. For example, "the number of hours the average American watches TV has remained steady, at about four and a half hours a day, every day (by age sixty-five, a person will have spent twelve uninterrupted years in front of the TV)."[12] These staggering statistics may have remained the same, but many things have been rapidly changing since Postman died.

Before he died, a new invention called the BlackBerry was still in its infancy. It was created in 1999 but did not attract much attention until 2004 when it finally reached its first million users. After taking five years to reach one million users, it only took ten months for the second million, then six months for the third million. In May 2009, there were an estimated 28.5 million BlackBerry users in the world. In 2007, Apple came out with the IPhone, which has revolutionized the phone technology market. IPhone is said to be close to the one billionth application downloaded.

Then there is social networking. Just about the time that Postman died, a college student created what is now known as Facebook. To date, there are over 300 million active users on Facebook, who spend a combined total of over six billion minutes each day on the site, which equates to just over three hours per day per person. There are forty million status updates each day. There are over two billion photos uploaded each month, as well as over two billion pieces of content (web links, new stories, blog posts, notes) shared each week.[13] In addition to Facebook, Twitter is growing in status. Beyond these technology updates, there are DVRs, HDTV (one wonders if Postman would have said the same about technology had he seen a good football game in HD), www.Hulu.com, (through which you can watch TV on the Internet), and text messages.

Can we all admit that technology is advancing so fast that it is difficult to keep up with the times? Many people love technology. I know I do. I am always running to the next appointment, wanting to redeem my time. So I make phone calls in the car. I wake up every morning

11. Postman, *Amusing Ourselves to Death*, ix.
12. Ibid., xiv.
13 Facebook Press Room, September 28, 2009, lines 1–12.

and check to see how many e-mails I have on my BlackBerry. I have my Twitter and Facebook accounts linked so that when I update one, the other automatically updates. Technology is awesome and helps me get the most done in a day. The only problem is that many people are now so accustomed to running at such a fast pace that when the sermon starts, sitting still and quiet is foreign to them and it is easy to lose concentration.

Timothy Turner, in his book *Preaching to Programmed People*, said technology has affected the way people listen to preaching. He called them "conditional listeners. Meet their conditions by giving them what they want and they'll listen. But when you don't, they tune you out."[14] We struggle with wanting to be entertained during the sermon. If the preacher is not funny enough or does not use enough high-tech videos, our listening is negatively affected. One piece of evidence Turner used to shows the subtle changes in our listening is what he called the consumer mentality to preaching. People with this attitude say things such as "'I am waiting for you to show me the benefits of your product. Make me want to listen. Create in me a demand.' Preachers can no longer count on a hearing for the Word of God based on its authority alone even in the church. The consumer mentality hungers to know, 'What will your product do for me?'"[15]

What does this mean for us? How can we overcome our natural tendencies so that we can enjoy technology but not be so consumed by it that it makes us bad listeners to sermons? One thing is not to be afraid of the silence. That may shock some of us who crave silence. For others, the thought of silence freaks us out. Actually, those who know me may laugh at this point; for I usually do not have silence. I have music playing all the time. As I write this, my ITunes is shuffling at full capacity.

But it is good at times to create silence. Turn everything off and just meditate and think. Spend some time alone. Go to the woods. Drive the car with nothing playing. Go golfing by yourself. Ride your motorcycle. Find something to do without any media influence. Andrew Postman told the story of a professor who in conjunction with the reading of his dad's book made her students engage in an e-media fast. For an entire twenty-four hours, the students were to refrain from all electronic media, including cell phones, computers, Internet, TVs, and car radios

14. Turner, *Preaching to Programmed People*, 38.
15. Ibid., 41.

among others.[16] That is a great idea! Try at some point to rid yourself of the media that has so affected our hearts.

A few months ago, I went on a wilderness leadership trip to Canada. For a guy who loves the city and despises camping, this was way outside my box. From Sunday morning to Friday night, I had no media influence in my life. I had no TV, no e-mail, no Fox news, no Sportscenter, no Facebook. Nothing! I had the company of some great men that I got to know but nothing technology driven. When our lives slow down like that, we get a chance to see what is really important. I realized how much I missed talking to my family. I realized how much I love talking to my God. I realized how much God loves to talk to me through his word. All of these things are often lost when my life becomes so technologically driven. Psalm 83:1 says, "O God, do not remain quiet; do not be silent." The thing is that God is not silent when the Scriptures are preached, but often our ears are so full from the technology in which we indulge that we think he is being quiet.

On September 27, 2009, Joshua Harris of Covenant Life Church preached a sermon entitled "Self-Control in a Wired World," trying to convince his people of the danger of being out of control with their technology. One text he dealt with was Proverbs 24:33–34: "A little sleep, a little slumber, a little folding of the hands to rest, then your poverty will come as a robber and your want like an armed man." In a blog article concerning his sermon, he said, "I focused on the issue of media, the Internet, and today's new technologies. I don't think I'm the only person who would identify this as an area where it's easy to lack self-control. I think a lot of us, we could rephrase the words of Proverbs 24:33–34 about the sluggard and say, "A little web surfing, a little Facebook, a little folding of the hands around the smart phone and spiritual poverty will come upon you like a robber."[17]

For our purposes, maybe it should be written this way: "A little web surfing, a little Facebook, a little folding of the hands around the smart phone and spiritual deafness will come upon us like a robber." If we want to overcome technology, let us make sure we are the ones using the technology, not the technology using us. Friends, let us overcome the technology age.

---

16. Postman, *Amusing Ourselves to Death*, xii.
17. Harris, "Self-Control in a Wired World," Lines 2–3.

OVERCOMING OUR TRADITIONS

Most people have traditions that they follow in their personal lives. There may be special things they do on Thanksgiving or during the Christmas season. Many times, traditions are handed down from parents to children. Other traditions are created; some are simply silly. When it comes to the church, although some traditions are good, many can be like cancer cells in the body. They can lay dormant for years and then all of a sudden become terminal.

Several months after Paul wrote his first letter to the church at Thessalonica, he wrote another letter. In this letter, he admonished the church concerning traditions: "But we should always give thanks to God for you, brethren beloved by the Lord, because God has chosen you from the beginning for salvation through sanctification by the Spirit and faith in the truth. It was for this He called you through our gospel, that you may gain the glory of our Lord Jesus Christ. So then, brethren, *stand firm and hold to the traditions which you were taught, whether by word of mouth or by letter from us*" (2 Thess 2:13–15, emphasis mine). Although these verses may be used by some hard-core fundamentalists who say that the Lord's Supper should only be taken on the first Sunday of the month because that's what they had always been taught, this text should not be used for that or for determining when the church should have potluck dinners. It refers to the teaching of the Scriptures.

Traditions here means "the things handed on." It denotes the teaching that is passed on from teacher to pupil. In context, it is clear that the emphasis is on the transmission of the gospel message. Therefore, when Paul talked about the traditions, he was talking about the *truth of the Gospel*! The fist needs to be clenched around this, not about allowing coffee in the worship center. It is to the message of the gospel that we must stand firm and hold on. False teaching will come and the false teachers will try to divert our attention away from what we have been taught, just as in Thessalonica. Paul was telling the people in that church that they must not forget the preaching of God's word.

However, some things that happen at church do not have anything to do with the gospel message or sound theology; yet we are tempted to hold onto them just as the Pharisees held onto their rules and regulations. Jesus called them hypocrites and said they honored him with their lips "but their heart is far away from Me. But in vain do they worship Me, teaching as doctrines the precepts of men. Neglecting the commandment of God, you hold to the tradition of men" (Mark 7:6–8). We must avoid the temptation to raise our preferences to the level of the gospel message and hold onto them with clenched fists.

This also is the solution for overcoming our traditions. Are they God's standards or are they our preferences? I am going to list several traditions that I see affecting listening to preaching. We need to ask if they are really biblical or simply our desires. Do we have a book, chapter, and verse in Scripture for them? Or have they simply always been done that way? As you read through these four traditions that we worry about, may you see the issues clearly enough to evaluate whether they are your preferences or God's standard.

First, stop worrying about the length of the sermon. I have a friend at a church who has been told he is only allowed to preach between twenty-five and thirty minutes. I am not saying that is a problem per se, but what if God has a longer message? To set time limits on sermons is a shallow view of preaching. Why does it have to end at a certain time? Why can't we just sit there realizing the privilege that God is speaking to us through the words of our preachers? This does not mean I advocate preachers preaching for two, three, or four hours at a time. But history has shown us that it is nothing to preach for forty-five minutes or even one hour. My fear is that when someone preaches longer than usual, we will shut down before he shuts down.

I am not much of a runner, but one thing I know is that a person needs to practice to build stamina. When I ran, I knew that by the second week I could run longer and stronger than the first week. The third week I could run longer and stronger than the second week and so on. The key was practice. Get over thinking the sermon has to be twenty minutes and work hard at listening so that, over time, listening for one hour will be nothing.

Struggles with the length of the sermon are also seen when preachers preach longer than they normally do. If church normally gets out at noon and the preacher is five minutes past, we get restless and shut down. We must resist turning off. We must resist looking at our watches, thinking that the restaurants are going to be full. Which is more important? The word of God or food? Job said, "I have not departed from the command of His lips; I have treasured the words of His mouth more than my necessary food" (Job 23:12). Mentally, decide that the word of

God is much more important to you than even the food that you need to survive in life, let alone another lunch at Chili's.

Second, stop worrying about what the preacher is wearing. There are some people I have met that say preachers should wear their Sunday best. That is how I grew up, always wearing my best clothes to church. As a preacher, I should be concerned about what I am wearing. I do not want to be a distraction in my clothing, but I also want to be comfortable in what I am wearing. Currently, I wear a suit or shirt and tie when I preach; but if it was up to me, I would not. I would dress nicely but not necessarily formally.

But as listeners, we should worry not about what the preachers are wearing but about what the preachers are saying. Some of the top heretics in the world are the best dressed (and smiling) people in the world. Conversely, some of the best preachers in the world do not own ties and would not be caught dead in Dockers. Remember, God said that he "sees not as man sees, for man looks at the outward appearance, but the Lord looks at the heart" (1 Sam 16:7). This is permission not to continue looking at the outward appearance but to develop the heart of God that looks at the heart of the man, not his clothing.

Third, stop worrying about the music that is sung before the sermon. Can the music before the sermon cause us to shut down and not want to listen to the preaching of God's word? Sure. I am well aware that good music can set the tone for good listening and bad music can be a hindrance to what is to follow. The truth of the matter is that there are very few churches that have good music, and even that is subject to everyone's interpretation.

I feel for men and women involved in music ministry, for it is the most volatile ministry in the church. For every fifty people in a church, there are fifty opinions on what songs should be sung, what style should be used, how many times songs should be repeated, and how many songs should be sung during a worship service. There are even some churches that do the bulk of their singing after the preaching of God's word (that would throw many of us into a tizzy!). In my church office today, we debated a certain song that was sung last Sunday. There were five of us involved in the conversation, and I do not think that anyone really agreed with anyone else. There will always be disagreement when it comes to the music ministry, but that does not mean that there needs to be distractions that lead to poor listening to sermons.

I mentioned in chapter 2 that it is helpful to sing what I call good, theological, soul-stirring songs. Music can be a fertilizer for the word of God, but it does not have to be a distraction. We had someone call our church the other day. They were new to our town and were looking for a church. Their only question was whether we sang only the "old hymns." We told them that we try to be balanced in our music and what should concern them more is the theology and preaching that a church holds, not the music. They did not want to hear that and were not swayed from their desire. It broke my heart because which is more important? The pregame or the actual game? Obviously, the actual game is what really matters. I am not trying to diminish the importance of singing songs in worship to our Lord and Savior Jesus Christ, but the sermon takes a priority in the service.

Let us not allow the style to get in our way. When we are singing a newer style that we do not like, think about the people who hated the style that we enjoy when it was introduced many years ago. Times change and we need to adapt. We probably need to evaluate our hearts to see if our style of worship is a form of idolatry to us. If we need a certain style to worship God, then it is idolatrous. When people next to us raise their hands in worship, rejoice that they apparently are entering into the throne room of God in worship through music and do not dismiss them as "one of those people." Ultimately, we need to decide if music is one of the issues on our to-die-for list. If it is, I feel for you. If it isn't, let it go and get ready for the word to be preached.

Fourth, stop worrying about the use of technology in the sermon. What if next Sunday our preachers use video illustrations to open their sermons? What will we do? What should our response be? Should we shut down and claim that our preachers are being influenced by the world; or should we sit there, watch, and look forward to their use of these illustrations to help us better understand God?

It has been mentioned several times already, but there are some people who really struggle with PowerPoint presentations. A few years ago, I was preaching at a church out of state on Colossians 1:15–20 concerning the greatness of Jesus Christ. That week I received an e-mail with some pictures of the earth in comparison to stars in our galaxy. I wanted to show that what we think is so big (the earth) is really small and that Jesus created them all. The pictures were to show the congregants the overwhelming power of Christ. When I proposed doing so to them, I was rejected. They thought showing pictures was not okay during the sermon. A few weeks later, I used those pictures at our church and they were greatly appreciated. I received several comments about how helpful these pictures were to people in realizing how big the galaxy is and how much bigger Jesus must be to have created it all.

Technology is one of those things that is a really touchy subject in many churches. At the center of the argument is the question of how much contextualization can be used in the church or in the sermon without corrupting the message of the truth that is being presented. One strong view is from Mark Driscoll, who is on the cutting edge of technology: "The church should not pursue innovative methods for the sake of coolness but for fruitfulness. Every church is culturally contextualized; the only difference is to what year."[18] He gave several examples of contextualization of the past. "As a general rule, Christians who attended church were expected to stand throughout the entire service. This began to change when some churches introduced benches in the thirteenth century and pews in the fourteenth century."[19] It was only in the fourteenth century that the first organ was put into a church. Some churches started to use organs for worship, and others totally rejected them as being from the devil.[20] He talked about the benefit of electricity, loudspeakers, and microphones for the benefit of the gospel. Radio and TV have changed the ways people can communicate the gospel message

It really frustrates me when preachers say they reject modern technologies as being worldly while they are sitting on their nice pews in well-lit auditoriums with high-class sound systems. A few years ago, I heard a preacher say that preachers should reject modern day technologies. He called them the techniques of the world. He was trying to make the point that the word of God is enough. I agree that the word of God is enough, but that does not mean that we should avoid all the technologies present today to communicate that Word? The funny thing about his sermon was that I was listening to him while sitting at my computer screen in Kansas. He was over 1,000 miles away. I was streaming him live. That was ironic.

So what is in and what is out? At this point, I defer to Matt Chandler, who gave this great advice at the Advance09 Conference in Durham,

---

18. Driscoll and Breshears, *Vintage Church*, 268.
19. Ibid., 269.
20. Ibid.

North Carolina, in June 2009 in a sermon called "Preaching the Gospel to the De-Churched": "Be creative. Men, if you want to use smokes and lasers and put a helicopter on stage that shoots a missile across the thing . . . if you can tie that back to the nature and character of God, I will not judge you. I will be in awe . . . but be faithful to the text and unpack God to your people."[21]

If our preachers unpack God to us, are faithful to the texts, have freedom to use some forms of technology, and do not lead us to sin, let them do so. Be thankful for preachers that care for us and the persons next to us. We cannot use the adage, "We have never done that before." It will just not do. Most of the stuff that we do in church at some point had never been done before. Friends, let us overcome our traditions.

The title of this chapter may have seemed funny to you. I am sure there are endless jokes that can be made about persevering the preaching of God's word. Unfortunately, this is not a joking matter. When preachers stand up and proclaim, "God says," it is serious business. We know that there are things in us and things that are around us that will try to stop us from hearing, listening, and obeying as we should. Let us overcome them all so at the end of any given Sunday, we can walk out of our churches saying, "God spoke to me today!" Amen? Amen!

---

21. Chandler, "Preaching the Gospel to the De-Churched," (June 4, 2009).

Conclusion

"THE WORLD IS DYING for want, not of good preaching but of good hearing."[1] My prayer is that this book is one step towards reaching that goal of good hearing. My perspective as I have been studying this issue for several years is that most people think they are good listeners to sermons. Recently I had the opportunity to get feedback from numerous individuals on their assessments of their own listening to preaching. Of these individuals, over 80 percent thought they were good listeners to sermons. I have to question whether or not their hearts have deceived them (Jer 17:9).

Personally, I have come to realize that I am not a great listener to sermons. There are times when I really hear from God, and there are times when I fail to hear what he is saying. How can I tell? I can tell through my actions. I can tell through my response. I can tell through the impact of the words that were spoken in my life. This is one area of my life that will always be a battle, as I am sure it will be for all of us.

However, there is a day coming when we will hear the voice of God and listen clearly and obediently at all times. It will start at the resurrection of our bodies. Jesus said, "An hour is coming, in which all who are in the tombs will hear His voice, and will come forth; those who did the good deeds to a resurrection of life, those who committed the evil deeds to a resurrection of judgment" (John 5:28–29). When Jesus said an "hour is coming," he was talking about a future event, which we know from other Scriptures is the resurrection of all people. There is coming a day when all the tombs will be opened, all will hear the voice of God, and they will come forth. When we come forth, there will no longer be any problems in hearing the voice of our Savior. There will no longer be any problems understanding what he desires for us. There will no longer be any distractions that will keep us from listening perfectly and obediently to him. Heaven will be like Adam and Eve in the Garden of Eden,

---

1. Lloyd-Jones, *Preaching and Preachers*, 122.

walking and talking and listening to God. Yet this time we will not rebel, we will not reject, we will not listen to the voice of another; we will only listen to the voice of God.

In June 1741, Jonathan Edwards preached a sermon at his church in Northampton, Massachusetts. It was a normal Sunday morning, and the people listened lethargically and left unaffected. Elizabeth Dodds recorded that the people "strolled outdoors to talk about whether the sunshine would hold up for the haying season."[2] Throughout this book, I have acknowledged that it is not uncommon for people to leave church talking about other things, even the weather. But what is interesting about this particular event is that this was not the last time that Edwards preached this sermon.

About a month later, Edwards was at a conference in Enfield, Connecticut. The scheduled preacher did not show up. Being asked to fill in, Edwards looked into his saddlebag and, on the spur of the moment, pulled out and preached "Sinners in the Hands of an Angry God." This sermon that had no effect on his church members became infamous to the little church in Enfield: "People 'yelled and shrieked, they rolled in the aisles, they crowded up into the pulpit and begged him to stop' . . . The people of Enfield that Sunday were in an expectant mood to hear the visiting preacher who was said to be famous even across the Atlantic Ocean. They did not take him for granted as Edwards' home church did. They did not hear him all the time, so they listened with fresh sensibilities. What he said slashed through to the hearers as a sermon seldom has in all of history."[3]

What always convicts me about that story is the thought of how many sermons my preacher has preached that are great, maybe even famous, sermons and I have been listening to another voice instead of listening to the voice of God.

The day is coming, friends, when we will no longer struggle. It is just around the corner. Until it comes, let us commit to preparing ourselves physically and spiritually for the preaching of God's word. Let us listen intently with a view toward the truth. Let us respond actively to the preaching each week, and let us fight to overcome obstacles that prevent us from listening to God as we should. Let us fight this battle

2. Dodds, *Marriage to a Difficult Man*, 92.
3. Ibid., 93.

together so that when the preacher stands up to preach, we will know what God is saying to us and will walk out different people.

Let me close with these urgent words penned by Richard Baxter: "Remember that you have but a little time to hear in; and you know not whether ever you shall hear again. Hear therefore as if it were your last. Think when you hear the calls of God, and the offers of grace, I know not but this may be my last: how would I hear if I were sure to die tomorrow? I am sure it will be ere long, and may be today for aught I know."[4]

---

4. Baxter, *Practical Works*, 475.

Bibliography

Adams, Jay E. *Be Careful How You Listen: How to Get the Most Out of a Sermon.* Birmingham, AL: Solid Ground, 2007.
———. *A Call for Discernment: Distinguishing Truth from Error in Today's Church.* Woodruff, SC: Timeless Texts, 1998.
———. *How to Help People Change.* Grand Rapids, MI: Zondervan, 1986.
Alcorn, Randy. *The Grace and Truth Paradox.* Sisters, OR: Multnomah, 2003.
———. *The Treasure Principle.* Sisters, OR: Multnomah, 2001.
Allen, Ronald J. *Hearing the Sermon.* St. Louis, MO: Chalice Press, 2004.
Anyabwile, Thabiti M. *What Is a Healthy Church Member?* Wheaton, IL: Crossway, 2008.
Armstrong, Lance. "Personal Information." No pages. Online: http://www.facebook.com/lancearmstrong.
Baxter, Richard. *The Practical Works of Richard Baxter*, vol. 1. Ligonier, PA: Soli Deo Gloria, 1990.
Bennett, Arthur, ed. *The Valley of Vision: A Collection of Puritan Prayers and Devotions.* Carlisle, PA: Banner of Truth, 1994.
Bock, Darrell L. *Luke.* Grand Rapids, MI: Baker, 1996.
Boice, James Montgomery. *Acts.* Grand Rapids, MI: Baker Books, 1997.
———. *The Gospel of Matthew*, vol. 1. Grand Rapids, MI: Baker, 2001
———. *The Gospel of John*, vol. 4. Grand Rapids, MI: Baker Books, 2005.
Brown, Colin, ed. *The New International Dictionary of New Testament Theology.* Vol. 2, G–Pre. Grand Rapids, MI: Zondervan, 1986.
Calvin, John. *John.* The Crossway Classic Commentaries. Edited by Alister McGrath and J. I. Packer. Wheaton, IL: Crossway, 1994.
Carter, Tom. *2200 Quotations from the Writings of Charles H. Spurgeon.* Grand Rapids, MI: Baker, 1988.
Challies, Tim. *The Discipline of Spiritual Discernment.* Wheaton, IL: Crossway, 2007.
Chandler, Matt. "Clouds on the Horizon." *9Marks eJournal* (May/June 2009). No pages. Online: http://www.9marks.org/CC/article/0,,PTID314526_CHID598014_CIID2475650,00.html.
———. "Preaching the Gospel to the De-Churched." Sermon, Advance09 Conference, Durham, NC, June 4, 2009. http://www.theresurgence.com/matt-chandler-preaching-gospel-de-churched (accessed January 29, 2010).
Davis, John J. and John C. Whitcomb. *Israel, From Conquest to Exile: A Commentary on Joshua–2 Kings.* Grand Rapids, MI: Baker, 1989.
Dodds, Elisabeth D. *Marriage to a Difficult Man.* Laurel, MS: Audubon, 2004.
Driscoll, Mark and Gerry Breshears. *Vintage Church: Timeless Truths and Timely Methods.* Wheaton, IL: Crossway, 2008.
Edwards, Jonathan. *The Works of Jonathan Edwards*, vol. 1. Peabody, MA: Hendrickson, 2005.

Bibliography

Fabarez, Michael. *Preaching That Changes Lives*. Eugene, OR: Wipf & Stock, 2005.

Facebook Press Room. No Pages. Online: http://www.facebook.com/press/info.php?statistics (accessed September 28, 2009).

Friedrich, Gerhard, ed. *Theological Dictionary of the New Testament*. Vol. 7. Translated by Geoffrey W. Bromiley. Grand Rapids, MI: Eerdmans, 1971.

Galli, Mark and Ted Olson. *131 Christians Everyone Should Know*. Nashville: Broadman & Holman, 2000.

Harris, Josh. "Self-Control in a Wired World." No Pages. Online: http://www.joshharris.com/2009/09/selfcontrol_in_a_wired_world_1.php.

Hendriksen, William. *Matthew*. New Testament Commentary. Grand Rapids, Michigan: Baker, 2004.

Hendriksen, William and Simon J. Kistemaker. *Thessalonians, the Pastorals, and Hebrews*. New Testament Commentary. Grand Rapids, MI: Baker, 2004.

Hiebert, D. Edmond. *James*. Chicago, IL: Moody, 1992.

The Holy Bible: Updated New American Standard. Anaheim, CA: Foundation Publications, 2003.

Hughes, Kent. *Disciplines of a Godly Man*. Wheaton, IL: Crossway, 1991.

Hughes, R. Kent and Bryan Chapell. *1 & 2 Timothy and Titus: To Guard the Deposit*. Preaching the Word. Wheaton, IL: Crossway, 2000.

Hybels, Bill. *Courageous Leadership*. Grand Rapids, MI: Zondervan, 2002.

Kent Jr., Homer A. *Faith That Works: Studies in the Epistle of James*. Winona Lake, IN: BMH, 1986.

Kesselman-Turkel, Judi and Franklynn Peterson. *Note-Taking Made Easy*. Madison, WI: The University of Wisconsin Press, 1982.

Kistemaker, Simon J. *1 Corinthians*. New Testament Commentary. Grand Rapids, MI: Baker, 2004.

Lawson, Steven J. *Famine in the Land: A Passionate Call for Expository Preaching*. Chicago, IL: Moody, 2003.

———. *Foundations of Grace, 1400 BC–AD 100. A Long Line of Godly Men*, vol. 1. Orlando, FL: Reformation Trust, 2006.

Lloyd-Jones, D. Martyn. *Preaching & Preachers*. Grand Rapids, MI: Zondervan, 1972.

Logan, Samuel T., ed. *The Preacher and Preaching: Reviving the Art in the Twentieth Century*. Phillipsburg, NJ: P & R, 1986.

MacArthur, John Jr. "Cultivating a Hunger for God's Word." No pages. Online: http://www.biblebb.com/files/MAC/80-174.htm.

———. *Ephesians*. The MacArthur New Testament Commentary. Chicago, IL: Moody, 1986.

———. *Hebrews*. The MacArthur New Testament Commentary. Chicago, IL: Moody, 1983.

———. *James*. The MacArthur New Testament Commentary. Chicago, IL: Moody, 1998.

———. *Reckless Faith: When the Church Loses Its Will to Discern*. Wheaton, IL: Crossway, 1994.

———. *Romans 1–8*. The MacArthur New Testament Commentary. Chicago: Moody, 1991.

———. *Romans 9–16*. The MacArthur New Testament Commentary. Chicago: Moody, 1994.

Mahaney, C. J. *Humility: True Greatness*. Sisters, OR: Multnomah, 2005.

Mayhue, Richard. *First and Second Thessalonians*. Focus on the Bible. Berkshire, Great Britain: Christian Focus, 1999.

Mohler Jr., R. Albert. "A Call for Theological Triage and Christian Maturity." No Pages. Online: http://www.albertmohler.com/?cat=Commentary&cdate=2004-05-20.
———. *He Is Not Silent: Preaching in a Postmodern World*. Chicago: Moody, 2008.
Moo, Douglas J. *The Epistle to the Romans*. NICNT. Grand Rapids, MI: Eerdmans, 1996.
Morris, Leon. *The First and Second Epistles to the Thessalonians*. NICNT. Grand Rapids, MI: Eerdmans, 1991.
Mulligan, Mary Alice and Ronald J. Allen. *Make the Word Come Alive: Lessons from Laity*. St. Louis, MO: Chalice, 2005.
Nichols, Ralph G. and Leonard A. Stevens. *Are You Listening?* New York: McGraw-Hill, 1957.
Nichols, Stephen J., ed. *Jonathan Edwards' Resolutions and Advice to Young Converts*. Phillipsburg, NJ: P & R, 2001.
Packer, J. I. *Knowing God*. 20th ed. Downers Grove, IL: InterVarsity, 1993.
Pink, Arthur W. *An Exposition of the Sermon on the Mount*. Grand Rapids, MI: Baker, 1994.
Postman, Neil. *Amusing Ourselves to Death*. 20th ed. London, England: Penguin, 2006.
Ramm, Bernard. *Protestant Biblical Interpretation*. Grand Rapids, MI: Baker, 1973.
Robertson, Archibald Thomas. *Word Pictures in the New Testament*, vol 5, *The Fourth Gospel, the Epistle to the Hebrews*. Nashville, TN: Boardman, 1932.
Ryle, J. C. *How Readest Thou: An Urgent Appeal to Search the Scriptures*. Moscow, ID: Charles Nolan, n.d.
Sarasin, Lynne Celli. *Learning Style Perspectives*. Madison, WI: Atwood, 1999.
Sarnataro, Barbara Russi. "Top 10 Fitness Facts: Some Things You Should Know about Exercise." No pages. Online: http://www.webmd.com/fitness-exercise/guide/exercise-benefits
Saucy, Robert L. *The Bible: Breathed from God*. Wheaton, IL: Victor Books, 1978.
Schultz, Thom and Joani Schultz. *The Dirt on Learning*. Loveland, CO: Group, 1999.
Smith M.D., Robert D. *The Christian Counselor's Medical Desk Reference*. Stanley, NC: Timeless Texts, 2000.
Spurgeon, C. H. *An All-Round Ministry*. Carlisle, PA: Banner of Truth, 2000.
———. *Lectures to My Students*. Grand Rapids, MI: Zondervan, 1954.
———. *The Treasury of David*. Updated by Roy H. Clarke. Nashville, TN: Thomas Nelson, 1997.
Stott, John R. W. *Between Two Worlds: The Challenge of Preaching Today*. Grand Rapids, MI: Eerdmans, 1982.
———. *The Contemporary Christian*. Downers Grove, IL: InterVarsity, 1992.
———. *The Message of Ephesians*. The Bible Speaks Today. Downers Grove, IL: InterVarsity, 1979.
Thomas, Robert L. *Revelation 1–7: An Exegetical Commentary*. Chicago, IL: Moody, 1992.
Tozer, A. W. *Whatever Happened to Worship: A Call to True Worship*. Camp Hill, PA: Christian Publications, 1985.
Turner, Timothy A. *Preaching to Programmed People: Effective Communication in a Media-Saturated Society*. Grand Rapids, MI: Kregel, 1995.
Whitefield, George. "Sermon 28: Directions How to Hear Sermons." No Pages. Online: http://www.reformed.org/documents/index.html?mainframe=/documents/Whitefield/WITF_028.html.